teach® yourself

italian
vocabulary
mike zollo
with alan wesson
and jane hughes
series editor
rosi mcnab

For over 60 years, more than
40 million people have learnt over
750 subjects the **teach yourself**
way, with impressive results.

be where you want to be
with **teach yourself**

For UK order enquiries: please contact Bookpoint Ltd, 130 Milton Park, Abingdon, Oxon OX14 4SB. Telephone: +44 (0) 1235 827720, Fax: +44 (0) 1235 400454. Lines are open 9.00–18.00, Monday to Saturday, with a 24-hour message answering service. Details about our titles and how to order are available at www.teachyourself.co.uk

For USA order enquiries: please contact McGraw-Hill Customer Services, P.O. Box 545, Blacklick, OH 43004-0545, USA. Telephone: 1-800-722-4726. Fax: 1-614-755-5645.

For Canada order enquiries: please contact McGraw-Hill Ryerson Ltd, 300 Water St, Whitby, Ontario L1N 9B6, Canada. Telephone: 905 430 5000. Fax: 905 430 5020.

Long renowned as the authoritative source for self-guided learning – with more than 30 million copies sold worldwide – the *Teach Yourself* series includes over 300 titles in the fields of languages, crafts, hobbies, business, computing and education.

British Library Cataloguing in Publication Data
A catalogue entry for this title is available from The British Library.

Library of Congress Catalog Card Number: On file

First published in UK 2003 by Hodder Headline Plc., 338 Euston Road, London, NW1 3BH.

First published in US 2003 by Contemporary Books, a Division of The McGraw-Hill Companies, 1 Prudential Plaza, 130 East Randolph Street, Chicago, Illinois 60601 USA.

Typeset by Transet Limited, Coventry, England.
Printed in Great Britain for Hodder & Stoughton Educational, a division of Hodder Headline Ltd, 338 Euston Road, London NW1 3BH by Cox & Wyman Ltd, Reading, Berkshire.

Impression number   10 9 8 7 6 5 4 3 2 1
Year   2008 2007 2006 2005 2004 2003

acknowledgements

I would like to thank the following for their help in producing this book: Jane Hughes, Alan Wesson and Paola Tite. As ever, I am also grateful to my wife and family for their patience and tolerance during the many hours I spent shut away with my computer.

contents

There have been many studies carried out into the way we learn vocabulary. The Swiss, who are generally acknowledged as experts in multi-language learning are also leaders in the understanding of the processes of language acquisition and some of their findings may be of interest to people wanting to broaden their vocabulary.

> Studies have shown that the most successful way [of learning vocabulary] is when the student is able to relate the new word to a concept and to integrate it into a conceptual system.
>
> (Wokusch, 1997)

Put simply this means that the most successful way of learning vocabulary is to put the new language into a context.

When a child first learns a language they are learning the concepts as well as the language at the same time. If you give a child an ice cream and say 'ice cream', they are learning the word and the concept at the same time, associating the word and the object. An adult has the advantage of already having the concept. An ice cream already conjures up other words: cold, vanilla, strawberry, like, don't like, size, price, etc.

Similarly if you decide to learn about a computer or a car you probably already know the parts or expressions you want to learn and can visualize them before you meet the word. In fact you already have the 'concept' and you can 'place' the new words within that concept.

It is for this reason that the vocabulary in this book has been given in context rather than, as in a dictionary, in alphabetical order. The words have been chosen as the words most likely to be useful or of interest to the learner.

One of the most useful tips in learning a new language is to look for ways of remembering a word: find a 'hook' to hang your new word or phrase on. We will now give you tips on how to make learning Italian words easier and more interesting.

How this book works

This book is more than just a list of words – it is a key to open the door to better communication. It is designed to give you the confidence you need to communicate better in Italian by increasing your knowledge of up-to-date vocabulary and at the same time showing you how to use the new words you are learning.

The first part of the book includes some useful learning tips, rules on pronunciation and shortcuts to look out for when learning new words. The toolbox provides you with the tools you need to speak a language. It includes basic information about the structure of the language and useful tips, including how to address people, how to ask questions, how to talk about what you have done and what you are going to do, useful expressions, and shortcuts to language learning. This part of the book is designed to be used for general reference.

The main part of the book is divided into topic areas: personal matters, family, work, education, etc. Most adults complain that they find it very difficult to learn vocabulary and wish they had learned it when they were younger. What they don't realize is that they are still trying to learn vocabulary in the same way as they did when they were children. The way the language is organized within the topic areas in this book is a direct result of studies carried out into language learning which show that adults find it difficult to learn long lists of words and find it easier to remember words if they are put into a context. It is for this reason that the vocabulary in this book has been given in context rather than, as in a dictionary, in alphabetical order. The selected words are the ones which our research has shown are the ones which are likely to be the most useful or most relevant to the learner of today. The words have been carefully arranged, grouped with other related words, nouns, verbs, adjectives, etc. and useful expressions with up-to-date notes about language fashions where relevant, so that the new language can be used immediately.

Make learning a list of words more interesting

- First decide which list you are going to look at today.
- See how many words you know already and tick them off.
- Choose which new words you want to learn. Don't try to do too many at once!
- Count them so you know how many you are going to try to learn.
- Say them aloud; you could even record yourself saying them.

Remembering new words

- Try to associate the new words with words that sound similar in English: *bicchiere beaker (glass)*.
- Try to associate the words with pictures or situations, e.g. try to imagine a picture of a rose when you say the word: **rosa**.
- See if you can you split the word into bits, some of which you know already: **super-mercato**.
- Look for words related to ones you know already: **giorno** (*day*), **giornale** (*daily, newspaper*); **pane** (*bread*), **panificio** (*baker's*).
- Look for words directly or indirectly related to the English ones: **bicicletta** (*bicycle*) **mano** (*hand* → *manual*).
- Learn the value of typical beginnings and endings used to alter the meaning of words: **impossibile** (*impossible*); **rimborsare** (*to reimburse*); **indipendenza** (*independence*); **capacità** (*capacity*).

Write words down

- Copy a list of the most important words onto A4 paper with a broad felt tip; stick it on the wall so that you can study it when doing household jobs or routine things such as washing up, ironing, shaving, or putting on make-up.
- For names of objects around the house, you could write the word on a sticky label or post-it note and attach it to the actual object.
- Copy lists of words in Italian and English in two columns. First, say each word aloud, then cover up one column, and try to remember each word in the other column.
- Do something else for half an hour and then come back and see how many you can still remember.

- Write down the first letter of each new word and put a dot for each missing letter, cover the word up and see if you can complete the word.
- Pick a few words you find difficult to remember: write each one down with the letters jumbled up; leave them for a while, then later try to unscramble each one.
- In your list, mark the difficult words: ask someone else to test you on the ones you have marked.

Spelling tips

- If a word begins with **f** + a vowel, try *ph*: **farmacia** *pharmacy*
- If a word begins with **t**, try *th*: **teatro** *theatre*
- Many words beginning with a vowel start with an **h** in English: **esitare** *to hesitate*
- Words with an *x* in English usually have **s** or **ss** in Italian: **tassì** *taxi*
- Italian does not have y; in the middle of a word it is replaced by **i**, and at the end of a word by -**ia**: **sistema** *system*; **geografia** *geography*
- For words beginning with **chi**, **fi** and **pi**, try English *cl*, *fl* or *pl*: **chiaro** *clear*; **fiamma** *flame*; **più** *plus*, *more*
- Some words with an **e** in Italian have an *i* in English and vice-versa, or even both: **prezzo** *price*; **dipende** *it depends*; **dieci** (*ten*, related to *decimal*)
- Where you see a word with the letters **uo** together, try replacing them with *o*: **uova** *egg* (related to *oval*); **ruolo** *role*
- Words which begin with **con-**, **dis-**, **im-**, **in-**, **re-/ri-**, **sub-** in Italian usually begin with *con-*, *dis-*, *im-*, *in-*, *re-*, *sub-* in English.
- Italian tends to simplify combinations of consonants, often doubling up the second one especially with -*ct*- and -*pt*- as follows: **ammiraglio** *admiral*; **attore** *actor*; **elicottero** *helicopter*.
- English words beginning with *constr-*, *instr-*, and *monstr-*, lose -*n* in Italian: **costruzione** *construction*
- Many words which end in -**abile** and -**ibile** in Italian usually have the same ending in English but without the middle vowel: -*able*, -*ible*. Other similar English–Italian endings are:

ending	example	ending	example
-aio	fornaio	-er	baker
-ore	attore	-or	actor
-mento	trattamento	-ment	treatment
-aggio	coraggio	-age	courage
-oso/a	generoso	-ous	generous
-ista	dentista	-ist	dentist
-zione	azione	-tion	action
-ale	razionale	-al	rational

Shortcuts: looking for patterns

Certain patterns reveal important facts about the type of word you are trying to learn.

- Most words in Italian ending in -o (except verbs) are masculine, belonging to the same group of words as real masculine words such as **ragazzo** (*boy*) and **toro** (*bull*).
- Most words in Italian ending in -a (except verbs) are feminine, belonging to the same group of words as real feminine words such as **ragazza** (*girl*) and **vacca** (*cow*).
- Most masculine words end in -o.
- Most feminine words end in -a.
- Words ending in -ore, -ere, -ale, -ile and -ame are masculine.
- Words ending in -ione, -udine, -igine, -ite, -ice, -i, -ie, -tù and -tà are feminine.
- Almost all verb forms end in a vowel.

Other patterns which can be seen in Italian are similar to those in English.

- Words ending in -mente (adverbs) are similar to English words ending in -ly, such as **rapidamente** *rapidly*; **costantemente** *constantly*. As you can see, in Italian and English, adverbs are based on adjectives, in this case **rapido** *rapid*, **costante** *constant*, simply with the endings -mente and -ly added.
- Sometimes, if you know a basic Italian word, it is easy to work out an adapted version.

  Here are some examples showing how this works:

-ale = -al	industria *industry*, **industriale** *industrial*	
-ore = -er	pittura *painting*, **pittore** *painter*	
-oso/a = -ous	favola *fable*, **favoloso** *fabulous*	
-ista = -ist	chitarra *guitar*, **chitarrista** *guitarist*	

- Similarly, some Italian words can be converted by adding a syllable at the beginning, and most work the same as in English, as follows:

con-	= *con-*	**tenere** *to hold*, **contenere** *to contain* (*hold within*)
re-	= *re-*	**inventare** *to invent*, **reinventare** *to reinvent*

- The following syllables added to the beginning of a word cause it to have the opposite or negative meaning:

dis-/des-	= *dis-*	**ordine** *order*, **disordine** *disorder*
im-	= *im-*	**possibile** *possible*, **impossibile** *impossible*
in-	= *in-*	**tollerante** *tolerant*, **intollerante** *intolerant*

The alphabet

This is the English alphabet with Italian pronunciation, useful if you need to spell out your name, surname, address and so on.

a	ah as in *car*
b	bi as in *beat*
c	chi as in *cheat*
d	di as in *deep*
e	e as in *egg*
f	effe as in *effective* but double length **f**
g	ji as in *genie*
h	acca as in *Acapulco* but double length **c**
i	ee as in *peep*
j	i lungo
k	kappa as in *cappa*
l	elle as in *telephone* but double length **l**
m	emme as in *emery* but double length **m**
n	enne as in *enemy* but double length **n**
o	o as in *cot*
p	pi as in *peep*
q	cu as in *cuckoo*
r	erre as in *hereditary*, with rolled **r**
s	esse as in *essential*
t	ti as in *teetotal*
u	oo as in *cuckoo*
v	vi as in *veeneck*
w	doppia vi as above
x	iks
y	ipsilon
z	dzeta

The letters *j, k, w, x* and *y* are not in the Italian alphabet and you won't find them in Italian words; however, they do figure in 'imported' words, and you may need to be able to spell them out if they appear in your personal details. Practise saying the letters of the alphabet aloud, and try spelling out your name, address and other important words.

Note that when spelling proper names over the phone, Italians use mainly names of towns: **A come Ancona, B come Bologna**, etc.

Ancona	i lunga / jersey	Savona / Sassari
Bologna	Kursaal / cappa	Torino
Como	Livorno	Udine
Domodossola	Milano	Venezia
Empoli	Napoli	Washington
Firenze	Otranto	ics / xilofono
Genova	Padova / Pisa	York / yacht / ipsilon
Hotel / acca	Quarto	Zara / zeta
Imola	Roma	

Punctuation

In addition to the pronunciation guide, you may need to say some of the following if you have to spell out something more complicated.

punctuation	punteggiatura
full stop	punto
comma	virgola
colon	due punti
semi-colon	punto e virgola
question mark	punto interrogativo
exclamation mark	punto esclamativo
inverted commas	virgolette
capital letter	maiuscola
small letter, lower case	minuscola
hyphen	trattino
dash	lineetta
full stop, new sentence	punto e segue
full stop, new paragraph/line	punto e a capo
next word	parola seguente
space	spazio
blank	spazio in bianco

forward slash	barra
backward slash	barra inversa
@ / at	chiocciola
computer keyboard	la tastiera
control	il tasto di controllo
alt	il tasto Alt
delete	il tasto di eliminazione
enter	il tasto di invio
return	il tasto di ritorno

Pronunciation

- Vowels: all are pure and always sound the same. All vowels are always pronounced, wherever they occur in a word. Where two or more vowels occur together, each is pronounced with its normal value in the correct order.

    e.g. italiano = italeeaaano
    macellaio = machellaeeo

- Consonants are always pronounced, wherever they occur in a word with one notable exception: **h**, which is **never** pronounced. Where they are doubled, you literally make them sound twice as long; this is what helps to give Italian its lilting, musical rhythm.

- Note and learn the pronunciation of the following consonants.

letters	sounds	examples
c	hard **c** before **a**, **o**, and **u**	casa, Como, cupola
	ch sound before **e** and **i**	Cinquecento, Cinzano, Gucci
g	hard **g** before **a**, **o** and **u**	gala, gola, guerra
	j sound before **e** and **i**	generale, Ginevra
ch	hard **c** before **e** and **i**	perché, chitarra, Chianti
gh	hard **g** before **e** and **i**	lunghezza, Lamborghini, ghiaccio
gl	*ly* sound	luglio, Gigli
gn	*ny* sound	lasagna, Mascagni, campagnolo
sc	*sh* sound before **e** and **i**	lasciare, scegliere, fascismo
q + u	pronounced as *kw* never as in French **qui**	questo
z	pronounced *ts*	zingaro (**ts**ingaro)
zz	pronounced *dz*	azzurro (a**dz**urro)

- Intonation is very sing-song, voice falls towards the end of a statement, and rises towards the end of a question.

- Stress: all words of more than one syllable have one stressed more than the rest. There are three hard and fast rules, but it is worth noting new words correctly and learning them with their stress pattern.

---

1 Most words of two or more syllables have the stress on the last but one syllable.

vino, madre, signore, ragazza, peperoni, televisione

2 Words with a written accent: the accent shows where the stress falls.

caffè, ragù, perché, giovedì

3 Words which don't follow rules 1 and 2 have to be learnt by experience!

gondola, sindaco, mi piacerebbero, telefonano

Written accents are also used to distinguish between pairs of otherwise identical words.

te	you	tè	tea
e	and	è	is
si	self	sì	yes

To sum up, once you are familiar with all of the above rules, Italian spelling and pronunciation are very reliable. Of course you won't learn them overnight, and it may be best to concentrate on learning and practising one at a time. Another useful method is to record and listen to spoken Italian as often as possible. Here are some ideas as to how you can make recordings of natural spoken Italian:

- Take a portable cassette player and some blank cassettes every time you go to Italy. Try recording from the local radio, or even people speaking, though you ought to ask their permission first!

- In some parts of the UK, especially in the south, you can sometimes pick up Italian radio: try playing around with your tuner, and if you find an Italian radio station, try to record some Italian.

- If you have Italian friends, ask them to make recordings for you, perhaps sending you messages with their family news, or giving you their views on topics of interest to you.

- If you have satellite TV, see if you can also receive Italian radio, and if not, talk to your local TV shop to ask if it is worth re-tuning your satellite equipment.
- Try to acquire recordings of Italian songs, pop music, ballads and so on – listen and learn!
- If you have access to the Internet, try to find Italian radio broadcasts, which are sometimes available via radio station websites.
- If you have Italian friends, try recording short messages on cassette, send them to your friends, and ask them to comment on, and correct your pronunciation.
- When speaking direct to Italian people, ask them to correct your pronunciation when possible.
- Once you have some recordings, listen to them as often as possible, and try to repeat what you hear, imitating the sounds and repeating short chunks of Italian. You might try writing out small sections, saying them aloud and comparing your version with the original.

toolbox

Nouns – gender and plurals

All Italian nouns (names of things or people) are either masculine or feminine, as explained on p. 5. Most end in -o (masculine) or -a (feminine), though there are a few exceptions to this rule and there are also other common masculine and feminine endings. Plurals are formed as follows: masculine words ending in -o change this ending to -i; feminine words ending in -a change to -e; words of either gender ending in -e change to -i. Words ending in other letters, including those ending in -è, -ì, -à or -ù generally have no separate plural ending.

There are a number of exceptions, best learnt separately; where possible the singular and plural forms of such exceptional words are given in this book. Adjectives behave in exactly the same way (see pp. 13–14).

libro / libri	*book / books*
rosa / rose	*rose / roses*
cognome / cognomi (m)	*surname / surnames*
chiave / chiavi (f)	*key / keys*
caffè / caffè (m)	*coffee / coffees*
lunedì / lunedì	*Monday / Mondays*
ragù / ragù (m)	*meat sauce / sauces*
città / città	*city / cities*

Many nouns, notably those referring to people, have specific masculine and feminine forms; some of these have been used in the following table to show typical masculine, feminine, singular and plural forms:

masculine singular	feminine singular	masculine plural	feminine plural
ragazzo	ragazza	raggazzi	ragazze
boy	*girl*	*boys*	*girls*
figlio	figlia	figli	figlie
son	*daughter*	*sons*	*daughters*
cugino	cugina	cugini	cugine
cousin	*(girl) cousin*	*cousins*	*(girl) cousins*
zio	zia	zii	zie
uncle	*aunt*	*aunts*	*aunts*
studente	studentessa	studenti	studentesse
student	*student*	*students*	*students*

Articles and other determiners

Nouns are often preceded by an article, in English either *the* (definite article) or *a / an* (indefinite article). There are more articles in Italian, because there are masculine, feminine, singular and plural forms as set out below. It is very useful to learn nouns with their definite or indefinite article, so that you know their gender:

un libro / il libro / i libri   *a book / the book / books*
una rosa / la rosa / le rose   *a rose / the rose / roses*
un pesce / il pesce / i pesci   *a fish / the fish / fishes*
una stazione / la stazione /   *a station / the station /*
  le stazioni   *stations*

Of course, nouns can have other so-called determiners (modifying words) in front of them, expressing possession or specifying which of two or more is referred to. Notice how, in the following table, nouns, articles and determiners are set out in columns: whichever column the noun is in, you can only use articles and determiners from that same column, so that they match the noun in gender and number. The table also includes a couple of adjectives to show how they fit into this pattern.

Here are some examples of how they are used:

Non è il mio amico, è il tuo.   *He's not my friend, he's yours.*
I nostri bambini più piccoli   *Our young children go to*
  vanno a questa scuola.   *this school.*
Non mi piace questo   *I don't like this dress;*
  vestito; preferisco quella   *I prefer that skirt.*
  gonna.

meaning	masculine singular	feminine singular	masculine plural	feminine plural
child / children	bambino	bambina	bambini	bambine
father(s) + mother(s)	padre	madre	padri	madri
old	vecchio	vecchia	vecchi	vecchie
young	giovane	giovane	giovani	giovani
the	il / l' / lo	la / l'	i / gli	le
a/an; some (in plural)	un / uno	una / un'	dei / degli	delle
my	il mio	la mia	i miei	le mie
your (familiar)	il tuo	la tua	i tuoi	le tue
his / her / its / your (formal)	il suo	la sua	i suoi	le sue
our	il nostro	la nostra	i nostri	le nostre
your	il vostro	la vostra	i vostri	le vostre
their	il loro	la loro	i loro	le loro
this / these	questo	questa	questi	queste
that / those	quel / quell' / quello	quella / quell'	quei / quegli	quelle

Adjectives

Adjectives are describing words which add information about nouns. They have to match the noun in gender and number, so they also follow the pattern set out in the previous table. Thus, in masculine form most adjectives end in -o, and in feminine form most end in -a; adjectives that end in -e can be used either with a masculine or a feminine noun without change; there are several other possible adjective endings. All adjectives form their plural according to the same pattern as nouns.

Unlike English, Italian usually places adjectives just after the noun they describe, but a few can go in front. They can also be used in other situations, such as after the verb *to be*.

il giardino grande	*the large garden*
la casa piccola	*the small house*
i meloni maturi	*the ripe melons*
le biciclette costose	*the expensive bikes*
il ragazzo è grasso	*the boy is fat*
le mele sono deliziose	*the apples are delicious*

The table on p. 13 shows how a couple of adjectives fit into the pattern of possible forms for nouns, adjectives, articles and determiners.

It is worth learning a few set phrases to help you remember the need for agreement and some typical endings.

masc. singular: un cavallo nero; il canal grande; questo libro interessante; il tuo vecchio amico

fem. singular: una casa bianca; l'isola bella; quella ragazza alta; la nostra amica intelligente

masc. plural: dei vini rossi; gli agenti segreti; quei ragazzi stupidi; i miei amici giovani

fem. plural: le donne eleganti; le terre fertili; queste pere mature; le loro case moderne

Here is a list of useful adjectives for describing people; remember, those ending in -o change to -a for the feminine form, and plurals are formed as in the table on p. 13; one or two are invariable (inv.), i.e. the same form is used for masculine and feminine:

tall / big	alto	*short*	basso
thin	magro	*fat*	grasso
old	vecchio / anziano	*young*	giovane
happy (contented)	contento	*sad*	triste
happy (nature)	felice / allegro	*unhappy*	infelice
quiet / shy	tranquillo	*open*	aperto
relaxed / laid back	rilassato	*stressed*	stressato
nice, pleasant	simpatico	*nasty*	antipatico
kind	gentile	*unhelpful*	poco disponibile
self-centred / egoistic	egoista (inv.)	*considerate / helpful*	premuroso
sporty / active	sportivo	*lazy*	pigro
good looking	bello	*ugly*	brutto
outstanding / exceptional	eccezionale	*ordinary / unremarkable*	ordinario / mediocre
smart	elegante	*scruffy*	trasandato
well-behaved	beneducato	*naughty*	cattivo
polite	educato	*rude*	maleducato

The following adjectives can be used to describe things:

old	vecchio	new	nuovo
good	buono	bad	cattivo
cheap	a buon mercato	expensive	caro
fast	veloce	slow	lento
in good condition	in buone condizioni	damaged	in cattive condizioni
flimsy	poco solido	solid	solido
rough	ruvido	smooth	liscio
shiny	lucido	matt	opaco
nice	piacevole	horrible	orribile
soft	morbido	hard	duro
interesting	interessante	boring	noioso

Often, we use adjectives to compare one thing or person with another, or with all others. To say something is ...-er than another, we use the comparative form of the adjective, and to say it is the ...-est, we use the superlative form. The comparative of most Italian adjectives is formed by simply putting **più** in front of the adjective, and the superlative uses **il/la/i/le più** in front of the adjective. Some examples can be seen in the following table. The Italian adjectives for *big*, *small*, *good* and *bad* can either be formed as described, or using special forms as given at the beginning of the table below.

adjective		comparative		superlative	
big	grande grandi	bigger	maggiore maggiori	biggest	il/la maggiore i/le maggiori
small	piccolo/a piccoli/e	smaller	minore minori	smallest	il/la minore i/le minori
good	buono/a buoni/e	better	migliore migliori	best	il/la migliore i/le migliori
bad	cattivo/a cattivi/e	worse	peggiore peggiori	worse	il/la peggiore i/le peggiori
ugly	brutto/a/ brutti/e	uglier	più brutto/a più brutti/e	ugliest	il più brutto/ la più brutta/ i più brutti/ le più brutte
useful	utile	more useful	più utile	most useful	il più utile la più utile i più utili le più utili

Verbs – infinitives and present tense

Verbs are words which describe actions, including abstract states or changes. Most verb forms tell you who is doing the action and when it is done, as well as what is being done (the **www** address of the verb!). Whilst in English, the **who** idea is expressed mostly by a person word (*I, you, he, she, it, we, they*) in front of the verb, in Italian the verb ending is enough to show this, and person words (subject pronouns) are only used when clarification or emphasis is needed. The subject pronouns are included in the tables below just for clarity. The verb endings also show **when** the action is done – past, present or future. Here are examples of the three main types of Italian verb in the **present** tense. The headings of the tables show the **infinitive** of the verb – the part of the verb without the person ending and the form found in dictionaries and wordlists meaning 'to ...'.

pronoun	**parlare** (infinitive)	*to speak*
io	parlo	*I speak*
tu*	parli	*you speak* (familiar)
lui / lei	parla	*he / she speaks*
		it speaks
Lei*		*you speak* (formal)
noi	parliamo	*we speak*
voi	parlate	*you speak* (familiar plural)
loro	parlano	*they speak*
Loro*		*you speak* (formal plural)

pronoun	**vendere** (infinitive)	*to sell*
io	vendo	*I sell*
tu*	vendi	*you sell* (familiar)
lui / lei	vende	*he / she sells*
		it sells
Lei*		*you sell* (formal)
noi	vendiamo	*we sell*
voi	vendete	*you sell* (familiar plural)
loro	vendono	*they sell*
Loro*		*you sell* (formal plural)

pronoun	**partire** (infinitive)	*to leave*
io	parto	*I leave*
tu*	parti	*you leave* (familiar)
lui / lei	parte	*he / she leaves*
		it leaves
Lei*		*you leave* (formal)
noi	partiamo	*we leave*
voi	partite	*you leave* (familiar plural)
loro	partono	*they leave*
Loro*		*you leave* (formal plural)

* **Lei** and **Loro** are the formal or polite ways of saying *you*, singular and plural. For historical reasons, they are used with the he/she/it form of the verb. The informal or familiar words for *you* are **tu** and **voi**. In most cases, strangers will address you as **Lei**, though when speaking to friends and younger people, **tu** is used. If in doubt, use **Lei** until and unless invited to use **tu**. In the plural, **voi** tends to be used for both familiar and formal.

Throughout this book when verb forms are translated, *you* is translated as either **tu** or **Lei**, depending on which is most likely for the expression translated; sometimes both are given, first the **tu** form, then the **Lei** form.

The *I* form is known as the first person singular, *you* as the second person singular, *he, she, it* as the third person singular, *we* as the first person plural, *you* (more than one person) as the second person plural, and *they* as the third person plural.

It is useful to learn these verb patterns by heart so that using them and choosing the correct one becomes automatic.

Here are the patterns for a few useful irregular verbs in the present tense:

essere* *to be*	**stare*** *to be*	**avere** *to have*	**andare** *to go*	**fare** *to do*
sono	sto	ho	vado	faccio
sei	stai	hai	vai	fai
è	sta	ha	va	fa
siamo	stiamo	abbiamo	andiamo	facciamo
siete	state	avete	andate	fate
sono	stanno	hanno	vanno	fanno

There are two verbs for *to be* in Italian: **essere** is used for permanent notions, often describing the essence of something or somebody; **stare** is used to describe what state somebody or something is in.

Here are the infinitives and first person (*I* form) of some other useful verbs. Note how the *I* form always ends in -o. In most cases, you can probably work out the other forms for yourself, but because some are less predictable (irregular) it is worth checking them in a good dictionary, grammar book or verb book.

to answer	rispondere, rispondo
to arrive	arrivare, arrivo
to ask	domandare, domando
to be able to	potere, posso
to bring / fetch	portare, porto
to call (phone)	chiamare, chiamo
to cancel	cancellare, cancello
to find	trovare, trovo
to forget	dimenticare, dimentico
to give	dare, do
to go in	entrare, entro
to go out	uscire, esco
to have to	dovere, devo
to know (a person, place)	conoscere, conosco
to know (a fact, how to ...)	sapere, so
to leave	partire, parto
to look for	cercare, cerco
to need	aver(e) bisogno di, ho bisogno di
to put	mettere, metto
to regret	essere desolato per, sono desolato per
to remember	ricordare, ricordo
to reserve / book	prenotare, prenoto
to see	vedere, vedo
to take	prendere, prendo
to want	volere, voglio
to write	scrivere, scrivo

Reflexive verbs

Reflexive verbs have a special 'person word' in front of them to describe actions which 'bounce back', affecting the person doing the action. In English, reflexive verbs have a 'self' word attached, i.e. *I wash myself*. Here is a typical reflexive verb set out in full; remember that the subject pronoun (in the first column) is not usually needed, but the reflexive pronoun (in the second column) is always used.

subject pronoun	reflexive pronoun	lavarsi (infinitive)	*to wash oneself*
io	mi	lavo	*I wash myself*
tu	ti	lavi	*you wash yourself* (familiar)
lui / lei	si	lava	*he / she washes himself / herself*
Lei			*you wash yourself* (formal)
noi	ci	laviamo	*we wash ourselves*
voi	vi	lavate	*you wash yourselves* (familiar plural)
loro	lavano		*they wash themselves*
Loro			*you wash yourselves* (formal plural)

Here are some more useful reflexive verbs. Notice the **si** attached to the end of the infinitive, which reminds you that the verb is reflexive. You will see that many reflexive verbs describe everyday routine actions we do to ourselves. The first person form of each verb is also given.

to wake up	svegliarsi	*I wake up*	mi sveglio
to get up	alzarsi	*I get up*	mi alzo
to wash oneself	lavarsi	*I wash myself*	mi lavo
to dress oneself	vestirsi	*I get dressed*	mi vesto
to have a shave	farsi la barba	*I have a shave*	mi faccio la barba
to comb one's hair	pettinarsi	*I comb my hair*	mi pettino
to put on make-up	truccarsi	*I put on make-up*	mi trucco
to have a bath	farsi il bagno	*I have a bath*	mi faccio il bagno
to go to sleep	addormentarsi	*I go to sleep*	mi addormento
to be called	chiamarsi	*I am called*	mi chiamo

The reflexive form of some other verbs is used to express the idea of *each other*: **ci vediamo ogni giorno** *we see each other every day*.

Talking about the past

Verbs have past tense forms to indicate actions which have already been done. There are two main past tenses in Italian: the perfect and the imperfect. The perfect is formed with the present tense of **avere** or **essere** and the past participle of the verb. The imperfect is formed by adding an ending to the stem of the infinitive. As an example, here are the imperfect and perfect tenses of **parlare** *to speak*.

tense	use	example	endings
perfect	single, completed actions in the distant or recent past	*I spoke,* *I have spoken*	ho parlato hai parlato ha parlato abbiamo parlato avete parlato hanno parlato
imperfect	ongoing, repeated actions and descriptions	*I was speaking,* *I used to speak*	parlavo parlavi parlava parlavamo parlavate parlavano

As you can see, for single, completed actions at a specific time in the past, you use the perfect tense (there is another tense with a similar use, but in spoken Italian most people use the perfect). You use the imperfect tense when you are talking about something that was happening, or used to happen, or for descriptions in the past.

Here are ten useful verbs in the perfect; note that some are based on the present tense of **avere**, others on the present tense of **essere**. As a rule, use **essere** with all reflexive verbs and with most verbs of movement. In case of doubt, the dictionary will give you the information.

infinitive	meaning	perfect tense	meaning
andare	*to go*	sono, sei, è andato/a siamo, siete, sono andati/e	*I went etc.*
venire	*to come*	sono, sei, è venuto/a siamo, siete, sono venuti/e	*I came etc.*
entrare	*to go in*	sono, sei, è entrato/a siamo, siete, sono entrati/e	*I entered etc.*
uscire	*to go out*	sono, sei, è uscito/a siamo, siete, sono usciti/e	*I went out etc.*
svegliarsi	*to wake up*	mi sono, ti sei, si è svegliato/a ci siamo, vi siete, si sono svegliati/e	*I woke up etc.*
alzarsi	*to get up*	mi sono, ti sei, si è alzato/a ci siamo, vi siete, si sono alzati/e	*I got up etc.*
divertirsi	*to enjoy yourself*	mi sono, ti sei, si è divertito/a ci siamo, vi siete, si sono divertiti/e	*I enjoyed myself etc.*
mangiare	*to eat*	ho, hai, ha, abbiamo, avete, hanno mangiato	*I ate etc.*
bere	*to drink*	ho, hai, ha, abbiamo, avete, hanno bevuto	*I drank etc.*
prendere	*to take*	ho, hai, ha, abbiamo, avete, hanno preso	*I took etc.*

Here are 15 useful verbs in the imperfect tense: only the first few are given in full, since, once you have the first person (*I* form), the remaining forms follow predictably:

I was etc.	ero, eri, era, eravamo, eravate, erano
I had etc.	avevo, avevi, aveva, avevamo, avevate, avevano
I was going etc.	andavo, andavi, andava, andavamo, andavate, andavano
I could etc.	potevo, potevi, poteva, potevamo, potevate, potevano
I was leaving etc.	partivo, partivi, partiva, partivamo, partivate, partivano

I was doing facevo, *I was working* lavoravo, *I was studying* studiavo, *I was eating* mangiavo, *I was enjoying myself* mi divertivo, *I used to live* vivevo, *I used to get up* mi alzavo, *I used to see* vedevo, *I used to want* volevo, *I used to know* sapevo.

Note the **-v-** in every form of the imperfect – the distinguishing feature of this tense.

Talking about the future

The future tense is formed by adding the appropriate endings to the whole infinitive or an adapted form of it. Therefore, its distinguishing feature is always an -r- before the appropriate ending. The endings are the same for all verbs without exception.

parlerò, parlerai, parlerà, parleremo, parlerete, parleranno

Here are some of the most commonly used verbs in the future tense; note that some have slight spelling changes to the infinitive, though the endings are all the same as those shown previously; only the first person form is given – you can work out the others from the pattern above.

to go	andare	*I will go*	andrò
to arrive	arrivare	*I will arrive*	arriverò
to know	sapere	*I will know*	saprò
to want	volere	*I will want*	vorrò
to go out	uscire	*I will go out*	uscirò
to put	mettere	*I will put*	metterò
to have	avere	*I will have*	avrò
to come	venire	*I will come*	verrò
to say	dire	*I will say*	dirò
to do	fare	*I will do*	farò

Here are some useful phrases in the future tense:

I will go – will you be going to the meeting?	Io ci andrò; tu ci andrai alla riunione?
I will do it. Will you do it?	Lo farò io. Lo farai tu?
Will you take the bus?	Prenderai l'autobus?
How will you go?	Come andrai?
When will you arrive?	A che ora arriverai?
When will you leave?	Quando partirai?
What will the weather be like?	Che tempo farà?
How much will it cost?	Quanto costerà?
Will it be suitable for children?	Sarà adatto ai bambini?
What will he do?	Che farà lui?
What will he have to drink?	Che prenderà lui da bere?
What will you take?	Che cosa porterai?
When will it be?	Quando sarà?
Is it going to rain? Or will it snow?	Pioverà, o nevicherà?
Will it be fine?	Farà bel tempo?
Will there be much traffic?	Ci sarà molto traffico?
There will be a lot of work.	Ci sarà molto lavoro.

Conditional and subjunctives

The conditional form of the verb is used to express wishes and possibilities. The endings are the same for all verbs.

farei, faresti, farebbe, faremmo, fareste, farebbero

You may have spotted that, as with the future, the ending is added to a stem based on the infinitive, therefore all forms have an -r- in them. Here are some useful expressions:

to prefer	preferire	Preferiresti un caffè? *Would you prefer a coffee?*
to want	volere	Vorrei andare al bar. *I would like to go to the bar.*
to like	piacere	Ti piacerebbe un aperitivo? *Would you like an aperitif?*
to be able to	potere	Lei potrebbe partire domani. *She could leave tomorrow.*
to go	andare	Andremmo se fosse possibile. *We would go if it were possible.*
to have	avere	Avresti abbastanza tempo? *Would you have enough time?*
to be	essere	Voi tutti sareste benvenuti. *You would all be welcome.*
to do	fare	Lo farebbero domani. *They would do it tomorrow.*

The subjunctive is a special verb form used where there is doubt or uncertainty, and for some command forms; it has its own forms and endings. Here are the endings of the present and imperfect subjunctive of the verb **essere**. Check regular -**are**, -**ere**, -**ire** subjunctive endings in a grammar or verb book.

sia, sia, sia, siamo, siate, siano
fossi, fossi, fosse, fossimo, foste, fossero

Here are some useful expressions using the subjunctive:

I think he is tired.	Credo che lui **sia** stanco.
He thought you were there.	Pensava che tu ci **fossi**.
Don't do that!	Non **faccia** così!
Speak more slowly, please!	**Parli** più piano, per favore!
Give me a kilo of sugar, please.	Mi **dia** un chilo di zucchero, per favore.
Tell me, where is the post office?	Mi **dica**, dov'è l'ufficio postale?

I *didn't want you to go out.*	Non volevo che tu uscissi.
I *am waiting for the train to arrive.*	Aspetto che **arrivi** il treno.
It *seems to us that the price has gone up.*	Ci sembra che il prezzo **sia aumentato.**

Negative expressions – saying you don't!

The Italian word **no** means *no* and **non** is used for *not*. Other negative expressions are given below, and **non** is used in front of the verb to introduce them. These negative expressions can also be used by themselves in front of the verb. Here are some examples.

Non mangio carne, non mi piace.	I *don't eat meat, I don't like it.*
No, non voglio uscire.	No, I *don't want to go out.*
Non ha niente.	He *has nothing. / He hasn't got anything.*
Non vale niente.	It *is not worth anything.*
Non ha visto nessuno.	She *saw nobody.*
Nessuno va a quel negozio.	No *one goes to that shop.*
Non lavoriamo mai a casa.	We *never work at home.*
Mai prendo l'autobus.	I *never go by bus.*
Non ho rotto nessuna finestra.	I *broke no windows.*
Non ha né famiglia né amici.	He *has neither family nor friends.*

Here are some further useful examples of negative expressions.

My *friend doesn't have a car.*	Il mio amico non ha una macchina.
I *don't have a bike.*	Non ho una bicicletta.
I *don't watch telly.*	Non guardo la tivù.
I *don't smoke.*	Non fumo.
I *don't go there any more.*	Non ci vado più.
I *won't see him / her any more.*	Non lo/la vedrò più.
I *don't play any more.*	Non gioco più.
Didn't *you book a table?*	Non hai prenotato un tavolo?
No, *they didn't answer the phone.*	No, non hanno risposto al telefono.
Didn't *you get to the bank?*	Non sei arrivato alla banca?
No, *it wasn't open.*	No, non era aperta.
Didn't *you speak to him?*	Non hai parlato con lui?
Didn't *you buy tickets for the match?*	Non hai comprato dei biglietti per la partita?

No, there weren't any left.	No, non c'erano più.
Didn't you see your friend?	Non hai visto il tuo amico?
No, he wasn't in.	No, non c'era.
Don't walk on the grass!	Non calpestare l'erba!
No entry	Vietato l'accesso
No exit	Vietato uscire
No admission for children	Vietato l'accesso ai bambini
No smoking	Vietato fumare
No dogs	Vietato l'accesso ai cani
Don't do it!	Non lo faccia!
Don't eat it!	Non lo mangi!
Don't open the window.	Non aprire la finestra.
Don't cross the road.	Vietato attraversare la strada.
.... is not allowed / permitted	non è permesso ...
not drinking water	acqua non potabile

Interrogative – asking questions

In English we sometimes ask questions by reversing the subject (person) and verb, so that, for example, the statement 'He is in a meeting' becomes 'Is he in a meeting?' as a question. In Italian this is not practical, because the subject pronoun is not usually used. In spoken Italian, the rise and fall of the voice (intonation) shows whether a question or a statement is intended – the voice rises at the end of a question, falls at the end of a statement. As a result, an ordinary sentence and a question can have the same words in the same order. Thus:

Parli inglese?	*Do you speak English?*
Parli inglese.	*You speak English.*
Ti piacciono le mele.	*You like apples.*
Ti piacciono le mele?	*Do you like apples?*

Here are some more examples of questions; the normal answer expected would begin with sì or **no**:

Did you go to town?	Sei andato in città?
Have you seen him?	Lo hai visto?
Did you try the steak?	Hai assaggiato la bistecca?
Have you seen the film?	Hai visto il film?
Can you drive a car?	Sai guidare la macchina?
Do you smoke?	Lei fuma?
Do you prefer red or white wine?	Preferisce vino rosso o bianco?
Do you eat fish?	Mangia pesce?
Are you taking medication?	Lei prende medicinali?

There are several words which can introduce a question, as you can see in the following examples:

Chi ha aperto la porta?	*Who opened the door?*
Che vuoi?	*What do you want?*
Che cosa hai in tasca?	*What have you got in your pocket?*
Cosa volete da mangiare?	*What do you want to eat?*
Come si chiama lei?	*What is her name?*
Perché fai questo?	*Why are you doing that?*
Perché lo vuoi?	*What do you want it for?*
Dov'è la tua amica?	*Where is your girlfriend?*
Quale libro vuoi?	*Which book do you want?*
Quali volete?	*Which ones would you like?*
Quando arriverà il treno?	*When will the train arrive?*
Di **quanti** soldi hai bisogno?	*How much money do you need?*
Quante mele vuole?	*How many apples do you want?*
Da **quanto** tempo sei qui?	*How long have you been here?*

Remember that you need to consider whether you are addressing the other person formally (**Lei**) or informally (**tu**) as this will affect the form of the verb.

Adverbs

You will remember that adjectives add information about nouns. In the same way, the main use of adverbs is to add information about actions. Many useful adverbs are based on adjectives. Just as in English we add -*ly* to the adjective, Italian adds -**mente** to the feminine form (if there is one – otherwise use the masculine). There are a few adverbs which don't follow this pattern: they are given first in the following table of useful adverbs.

adjective	meaning	adverb	meaning
		molto	*very*
		abbastanza	*quite*
buono	*good*	bene	*well*
cattivo	*bad*	male	*badly*
precedente	*previous*	prima	*previously*
in anticipo	*early*	presto	*early*
in ritardo	*late*	tardi	*late*
veloce	*quick, fast, rapid*	velocemente	*quickly, fastly, rapidly*
lento	*slow*	lentamente	*slowly*

immediato	*immediate*	immediatamente	*immediately*
completo	*complete*	completamente	*completely*
improvviso	*sudden*	improvvisamente	*suddenly*
silenzioso	*noiseless*	silenziosamente	*noiselessly*
conveniente	*convenient*	convenientemente	*conveniently*
tecnico	*technical*	tecnicamente	*technically*
triste	*sad*	tristemente	*sadly*
frequente	*frequent*	frequentemente	*frequently*
raro	*rare*	raramente	*rarely*
prossimo	*next*	prossimamente	*next*

Here are some additional adverbs and adverbial phrases, which do not fit into any pattern:

ogni tanto	*occasionally*
qualche volta	*sometimes*
spesso	*often*
molto spesso	*very often*
adesso	*now*
già	*already*
presto	*soon*
prima	*before*
dopo	*afterwards*
poi	*then*
un poco	*a little*

Just like adjectives, adverbs can also have comparative and superlative forms. They are formed in the same way, as shown in the first two examples in the following table; note also the special forms based on **bene** and **male**.

adverb	comparative	superlative
velocemente	più velocemente	il più velocemente (possibile)
fast	*faster*	*fastest*
lentamente	più lentamente	il più lentamente (possibile)
slowly	*slower*	*slowest*
bene	meglio	il meglio (possibile)
well	*better*	*best*
male	peggio	il peggio (possibile)
badly	*worse*	*worst*

Colours and sizes

Colours *i colori*

Here is a list of common colours. Remember, these are all adjectives, so they go after the noun and follow the usual rules of agreement with nouns. To remind you, those ending in -o also have endings in -a, -i and -e; those ending in -e just have a plural ending in -i. There are also three which are invariable, marked (inv.), which don't change at all.

black	nero
blue	azzurro / blu (inv.)
brown	marrone
green	verde
grey	grigio
mauve	malva (inv.)
orange	arancione
pink	rosa (inv.)
purple	viola (inv.)
red	rosso
white	bianco
yellow	giallo

Here are examples of colours in use:

a red car	una macchina rossa
a black suit	un abito nero
a pink jumper	un maglione rosa
a pink blouse	una camicetta rosa
a blue shirt	una camicia azzurra
blue trainers	scarpe da ginnastica azzurre/ blu
grey shoes	scarpe grigie
brown gloves	guanti marroni

Finally, here is a list of most of the other colours you are likely to need.

blue-grey	grigiazzurro
light / pale blue	azzurro chiaro / celeste
dark blue	azzurro scuro / blu (inv.)
cream / ivory	color crema (inv.)
salmon pink	rosa salmone (inv.)
fuchsia	fucsia (inv.)
khaki	cachi (inv.)
burgundy	granata (inv.)
lilac	lilla (inv.)
navy blue	blu scuro

royal blue	azzurro reale
pale green	verde chiaro
dark green	verde scuro
olive green	verde oliva (inv.)
bright red	rosso acceso
scarlet	scarlatto
beige	beige (inv.)
emerald	verde smeraldo
ruby	(color) rubino (inv.)
sapphire	blu zaffiro (inv.)
turquoise	(color) turchese (inv.)

Sizes *le misure e le taglie*

Sizes too are adjectives, and follow the normal rules on position and agreement.

very small	molto piccolo
small	piccolo
medium	medio
average	medio
large	grande
very large	molto grande
wide	largo
narrow	stretto
long	lungo
short (objects)	corto
short (people)	basso / piccolo

Numbers, days, dates and times

Cardinal numbers *i numeri cardinali*

1	uno/una	13	tredici	25	venticinque
2	due	14	quattordici	26	ventisei
3	tre	15	quindici	27	ventisette
4	quattro	16	sedici	28	ventotto
5	cinque	17	diciassette	29	ventinove
6	sei	18	diciotto	30	trenta
7	sette	19	diciannove	31	trentuno/a
8	otto	20	venti	40	quaranta
9	nove	21	ventuno/a	50	cinquanta
10	dieci	22	ventidue	60	sessanta
11	undici	23	ventitré	70	settanta
12	dodici	24	ventiquattro	80	ottanta

90	novanta	1,000	mille
100	cento	2,000	duemila
101	centouno	2,100	duemilacento
102	centodue	5,000	cinquemila
110	centodieci	10,000	diecimila
150	centocinquanta	million	un milione
200	duecento	billion	un miliardo
300	trecento		
400	quattrocento		
500	cinquecento		

- Numbers written as figures are just as in English, except that 7 is always crossed 7.
- When saying a long number aloud, such as a telephone number, Italians either say each number individually or split the numbers into pairs, as in this example; note that if there is an odd number, the first three may be expressed as hundreds.

    9865423 = nove-otto-sei-cinque-quattro-due-tre

    or novecentoottantasei, cinquantaquattro, ventitré

- In Italian usage, as in most other European countries, a full stop is used to indicate thousands instead of a comma, and a comma is used where we use a decimal point.

    tremiladuecentoquindici = 3.215

    sedici virgola quattro = 16,4

Ordinal numbers *i numeri ordinali*

These are adjectives ... so remember the rules!

first	primo
second	secondo
third	terzo
fourth	quarto
fifth	quinto
sixth	sesto
seventh	settimo
eighth	ottavo
ninth	nono
tenth	decimo
21st	ventunesimo
21st birthday	il ventunesimo compleanno

Here are some fractions.

half	la metà
third	il terzo
quarter	il quarto
fifth	il quinto

Years and centuries *gli anni e i secoli*

the century	il secolo
the 1500s	il Cinquecento
the 1900s	il Novecento, il ventesimo secolo
the 20th century	il ventesimo secolo
the 21st century	il ventunesimo secolo
the 22nd century	il ventiduesimo secolo
the millennium	il millennio
the 1990s	gli anni novanta
the year 2000	l'anno duemila
the year 2010	l'anno duemiladieci
next year	l'anno prossimo
last year	l'anno scorso
the year before last	due anni fa
the year after next	fra due anni

Days and months *i giorni e i mesi*

In Italian, days of the week and months of the year are written with a small letter, except when they start a sentence. They are all masculine except **la domenica**.

Monday	lunedì	*Saturday*	sabato
Tuesday	martedì	*Sunday*	domenica
Wednesday	mercoledì	*on Thursday*	giovedì
Thursday	giovedì	*on Saturdays*	il sabato
Friday	venerdì		

January	gennaio	*July*	luglio
February	febbraio	*August*	agosto
March	marzo	*September*	settembre
April	aprile	*October*	ottobre
May	maggio	*November*	novembre
June	giugno	*December*	dicembre

Expressions of time *espressioni di tempo*

day	il giorno
week	la settimana
month	il mese
year	l'anno
last year / month	l'anno / il mese scorso
last week	la settimana scorsa
next week	la settimana prossima
next month / year	il mese / l'anno prossimo
yesterday	ieri
the day before yesterday	l'altro ieri
today	oggi
tomorrow	domani
the day after tomorrow	dopodomani
early morning	al mattino presto
morning	la mattina
afternoon	il pomeriggio
evening	la sera
night	la notte
tomorrow morning	domani mattina
yesterday afternoon	ieri pomeriggio
this afternoon	questo pomeriggio
tonight	stasera

Dates *le date*

2nd April	il due aprile
31st July	il trentun luglio
1st December	il primo dicembre
8th February	l'otto febbraio

To express dates in Italian, use the masculine article followed by the cardinal number, and then the month. Use the ordinal number only for the first day of the month, e.g. **il primo giugno**. When mentioning the day of the week in the date, Italian drops the article, e.g. **lunedì otto maggio**.

The seasons *le stagioni*

spring	la primavera
summer	l'estate
autumn	l'autunno
winter	l'inverno

The clock l'orologio

What time is it?	Che ora è? / Che ore sono?
midday midnight	è mezzogiorno / mezzanotte
1 o'clock	è l'una
2 o'clock	sono le due
3.05	sono le tre e cinque
4.10	sono le quattro e dieci
5.15	sono le cinque e un quarto
6.20	sono le sei e venti
7.25	sono le sette e venticinque
8.30	sono le otto e mezzo / mezza
9.35	sono le dieci meno venticinque
10.40	sono le undici meno venti
11.45	sono le dodici meno un quarto
12.50	è l'una meno dieci
13.55	sono le due meno cinque

You can see that Italian uses è before 1 o'clock, midday and midnight, which is quite logical since all are singular, then **sono le** for the rest, which are plural. You will also by now have worked out that from the hour to half past, you simply add **e** and the number, **un quarto** or **mezzo/a**, and then use **meno** from half past up to the hour, calculating backwards from the next hour as in English. You can also add **di/della mattina, di/del pomeriggio, di sera** and **di notte** if you want to be precise, such as in the example:

It is four o'clock in the afternoon.	Sono le quattro di pomeriggio.

The 24-hour clock is also used very widely in Italy, especially on the radio and for transport. In these instances the times are expressed pretty much as in English:

It is 0900 hours.	Sono le ore zero nove.
It is 1315.	Sono le tredici e quindici.
It is 2245.	Sono le ventidue e quarantacinque.

Finally, some extra vocabulary and expressions to do with time:

second	il secondo
minute	il minuto
hour	l'ora
half hour	la mezz'ora

clock, watch	l'orologio
alarm clock	la sveglia
early	presto
late	tardi
sooner or later	prima o poi
Better late than never!	Meglio tardi che mai!
telling the time	dire l'ora
my watch has stopped	si è fermato il mio orologio
is (... minutes) fast	va avanti (di ... minuti)
is (... minutes) slow	è indietro di ... minuti
sunset	il tramonto
sunrise	lo spuntar del sole
dawn / daybreak	l'alba
dusk / nightfall	il crepuscolo

Quantity

weight	il peso
height	l'altezza / la statura
length	la lunghezza
size	la taglia / la misura

Weights and measures *pesi e misure*

kilo	il chilo
half a kilo	il mezzo chilo
500 grammes	cinquecento grammi / mezzo chilo
a pound	una libbra
a litre	un litro
a metre	un metro
a centimetre	un centimetro
a kilometre	un chilometro
a pair	un paio
a dozen	una dozzina
bottle	una bottiglia
jar	un vasetto
tin	una scatola
box	una scatola / lattina
pot	un vasetto
package	un pacco

lots of (e.g. sugar)	molto (zucchero)
lots of (e.g. meat)	molta (carne)
lots of (e.g. lemons)	molti (limoni)
lots of (e.g. apples)	molte (mele)
a little ...	un poco di ... / un po' di
a few ...	alcuni/e ...
more of	più di ...
a portion of	una porzione di
about 10	una decina
about 15	una quindicina
about 20	una ventina
about 100	un centinaio
about 1000	un migliaio

Exclamations, giving orders, being polite

How to say *please* and *thank you!*

Thank you	Grazie!
Please	Per favore / per piacere / per cortesia

You will find that Italians say *don't mention it* far more often than we do: **prego!**

Giving orders / commands

You will remember that Italian has four ways of saying *you*: familiar singular (**tu**), polite singular (**Lei**), plural (**voi**) and 'extra-polite' plural (**Loro**). Look back to page 17 to remind yourself when to use each form. In general, when giving orders to strangers you should use the formal or polite form.

Help!	Aiuto!
Fire!	Al fuoco!
Cheers! (with drink)	Salute! / Cin, cin!
Cheers! (thanks)	Grazie
Cheers (Goodbye)	Ciao!
Cheerio	Ciao!
Please	Per favore / per piacere / per cortesia

Wait!	Aspetta! / Aspetti!
Stop!	Fermati! / Si fermi!
Listen!	Ascolta! / Ascolti!
Look!	Guarda! / Guardi!
Pass me a knife	Dammi / Mi dia un coltello
Fetch a glass	Portami / Mi porti un bicchiere
Take the chocolates	Prendi / Prenda i cioccolatini
Bring me my bag	Portami / Mi porti la mia borsa
Excuse me (listen to me)	Senti / Senta
Excuse me (sorry)	Scusami / (Mi) scusi
Excuse me (I want to pass)	Permesso
I'm sorry	Scusami / Mi scusi
I didn't mean it	Non intendevo farlo
I didn't know	Non lo sapevo
I didn't understand	Non capivo
Sorry I'm late	Scusami / Mi scusi per il ritardo

Being polite

Yes, please	Sì, grazie
No, thank you	No, grazie
Don't mention it	Prego
Not at all	Prego
Pardon? (please repeat)	Come?
I didn't catch what you said	Non ho afferrato bene quello che ha detto
I don't understand	Non capisco / Non ho capito
Can I help you?	Desidera?
Can you help me?	Mi può aiutare?
Can you say it again?	Può ripetere, per favore?
Can you speak more slowly, please?	Parli più lentamente, per favore.
Please will you write it down?	Per favore, lo metta per iscritto.

Italian spelling quirks

This section helps you with the 'spelling quirks' of Italian, and the peculiarities of Italian punctuation. First a few general points:

• Almost all Italian words end in vowels; a handful of consonants occur at the end of words, but relatively rarely. Italian does not like complicated combinations of consonants and often goes for simplified spellings compared to other languages; however, double consonants (two of the same) are common.

- In Italian accents are only ever put on a final vowel: they do not alter the sound of the letter that carries one, but the syllable in which it occurs is pronounced more loudly than the rest of the word.

- As you have seen on p. 31, Italian uses capital letters less than English, notably not on names of days and months, nationalities and names of languages.

- Punctuation is mostly the same as in English, except as related to numbers, as seen on p. 30.

- Italian intonation has quite a 'sing-song' nature anyway, but remember that in a question the voice rises towards the end, whilst in a normal statement, it rises before a comma, but falls at a colon, semi-colon or full stop. In an exclamation, the most important words are spoken with more emphasis.

Recognizing Italian words

- Modern Italian is derived from the Latin spoken by ordinary Romans. Much vocabulary in English also comes from Latin, either via Norman French, from other Romance languages, or directly from Latin in more recent times (largely in the fields of science or culture). Hence, Italian and English have a lot of vocabulary in common, and many words new to you in Italian will be recognizable via English or any other Romance language you happen to know.

- Italian has also imported words from many other languages over the centuries, including a lot from English, especially in recent years (e.g. *design, gadget, computer*), mostly in the fields of sport, pop music, business, science and computing. Some imported words keep more or less their original spelling, only sometimes with Italian pronunciation: this is usually the case with words adopted in written form, e.g. *design*. Words imported through spoken language tend to adapt to keep the pronunciation similar: such is the case with **gol, scuter**. Sometimes Italian even "re-invents" an English word, such as **footing**, which we would not use in English to mean *jogging*. It is worth noting that verbs based on imported words tend to be in the **-are** verb family, e.g. **filmare, fotocopiare**.

- New words should not always send you rushing for a dictionary. Often, you will be able to work out the likely meaning from experience, especially if you already know the base word at the core of the new word, or recognize it through English or another language you know. (But beware of "falsi amici", which look the same but are not!) The next two sections will help you to make informed guesses.

Cognates

Cognates are words which come from a common source, and so the meaning of the Italian version should be easy to guess; they can usefully be categorized as follows:

- English words absorbed into Italian without change of meaning:

    shopping, design, marketing, scuter, gol

    Some, like the last two, have spellings 'adapted' into Italian to 'sound' as in English.

- Italian words with common equivalent in English, or English words borrowed from Italian:

    pasta, vino, allegro, concerto

- Words identical in form to their English equivalent and with comparable pronunciation:

    panorama, idea

- Words similar in form to their English equivalent and with comparable pronunciation:

    documento, militare, sistema, clima, movimento, originale

- Verbs whose stem is identical or similar in form to the English equivalent:

    ammirare, contenere, consistere

- Words containing certain frequently occurring Italian orthographic features which, once known, allow ready identification with English equivalents:

    libertà, turismo, indicazione, potenza

Note the equivalent English – Italian suffixes:

-tà = -ty	**città** *city*; **capacità** *capacity*
-zione = -tion	**azione** *action*; **elezione** *election*
-ia = -y	**energia** *energy*; **farmacia** *pharmacy*

Many other prefixes and suffixes can be added to this list.

Derivatives

In both written and spoken Italian, 'undressing' a new word to get at its core often makes it recognizable. It helps to bear in mind plural forms of nouns, adjectival agreement and verb forms, and the basic principles by which these are used. Here are some basic categories of derivative:

- Words whose meaning is determined by common prefixes or suffixes, but with a known or identifiable base form:

    con-: contenere, conseguenza
    s-: sfortuna, snazionalizzare
    dis-: dissuadere, dispensare
    in-/im-: incorrotto, impossibile
    re-/ri-: reversibile, ricominciare
    sub-: subaffittare, subcosciente
    -abile: nota → notabile
    -eria: pasta → pasticceria
    -mento: inquinare → inquinamento
    -oso: arena → arenoso, noia → noioso

- Nouns denoting people and other related concepts, which are characterized by endings such as **-aio/a, -ore/rice, -ista, -eria**:

    -aio/-aia: tabaccaio
    -ista: pianista, tassista
    -ore/-rice: pittore / pittrice, attore / attrice
    -eria: pizzeria, salumeria

    These are mostly based on another noun or a verb.

- Adverbs formed by adding the ending **-mente** to known or easily identifiable adjectives:

    totalmente, attivamente

    Most adverbs end in **-mente,** just as in English most end in *-ly*.

- Adjectives with ending **-abile** or **-ibile** which compare with English equivalents ending in *-able* or *-ible* deriving from easily known or identifiable words:

    immaginabile, ammirabile

- Adjectives with ending **-oso/-osa** comparable with English equivalents ending in *-ous*, and which are easily identifiable:

    religioso, furioso, vigoroso, vizioso

- Adjectives with ending **-ese, -ino/a, -ano/a** comparing with English *-ese* or *-(i)an*, usually indicating place of origin:

    inglese, giapponese, canadese, fiorentino, napoletano

- Diminutives such as words ending in **-etto/a**, **-ino/a** deriving from known or other easily identifiable words.

     signorino, panino, bellino, fioretta

- Augmentative and pejorative suffixes such as **-one/ona**, **-azzo**, **-accio/uccio**:

     filmaccio, erroraccio, cenone

- Compound nouns, consisting of combinations of known words; these often consist of verb and plural form of the noun object of the action implied:

     apriscatole, portacenere, lavastoviglie

- Words derived from adjectives:

     tranquillizzare, pulizia

- Words mainly derived from verbs, with endings **-ante** or **-ente**:

     cantante, agente

- Place names with identical or similar spelling to English equivalent:

     Italia, America, Brasile

- Common acronyms and initials (often in a different order):

     NATO   *NATO*

     ONU – Organizzazzione delle
                    Nazioni Unite   *UN – United Nations*
     UE – Unione Europea   *EU – European Union*

01

personal matters

1.1 Titles, greetings and making arrangements

Core vocabulary

titles *titoli*

Mr	signor (Sig.)
Mrs	signora (Sig.ra)
Miss	signorina (Sig.rina)
Sir	Signore
Madam	Signora

ℹ️ Signore is used for both *Mr* and *Sir*; the latter is used to a stranger by, for example, a shop assistant, and by a serviceman to a senior officer; **signora** is used for both *Mrs* and *Madam* in the same way, and **signorina** is always used for *Miss*. All of these are used with the person's surname, whether or not their first name is also being used, and are preceded with **il** or **la** except when you are speaking direct to *him / her*:

il signor Bianchi; la signora Colombo;
'Buongiorno signorina Borelli'.

Italian also has another courtesy title – **don / donna**: this is only really used in southern Italy and Sicily, and is reserved for someone of some status or age, being placed in front of the person's first name.

don Antonio; donna Maria

Italian people usually use **dottor(e)** when referring to or addressing a doctor, even though the normal word for the profession is **medico**. They also address as **dottor(e)** anybody who has graduated from university and any person in a senior position. A lawyer is referred to as **avvocato**, teachers can be addressed as **professore** and engineers are often referred to as **ingegnere**. The abbreviations used in front of the person's name when written are: **Dott.**, **Avv.**, **Prof.**, and **Ing**. The normal word for boss is **padrone**.

greetings *saluti*

Hello, hi	Ciao!
Good morning	Buongiorno
Good afternoon, *Good evening*	Buona sera
Good night	Buona notte
Goodbye	Arrivederci / Ciao (informal)

i Note that **sera** is used both for late *afternoon* and *evening*, and lasts from approximately 5 p.m. to midnight. **Buona notte** can be used only when you are leaving someone late in the evening, to go home or to bed.

introducing someone *presentare qualcuno*

This is ...	Questo è ...
May I introduce ...?	Ti/Le presento ...
Are you (Mr ...)?	Lei è ...?
Do you know (Mr ...)?	Conosce ...?
Mr What's-his-name	il Signor Coso
Mrs What's-her-name	la Signora Cosa
Pleased to meet you	Piacere (di conoscerla)
May I sit here?	Posso sedermi qui?
Are you alone?	Lei è solo / sola?

I am ... *Sono ... / Mi chiamo ...*

single	celibe (male) / nubile (female)
married	sposato/a
divorced	divorziato/a
separated	separato/a
a widow	vedova
a widower	vedovo

making arrangements *organizzare qualcosa*

What shall we do this evening?	Che cosa facciamo stasera?
Hello	Ciao! (familiar) / Buon giorno! (formal)
May I introduce myself?	Mi presento
This is my wife/husband/ friend	Ti/Le presento mia moglie / mio marito / il mio amico / la mia amica
Pleased to meet you	Molto lieto / piacere!
May I sit here?	Posso sedermi qui?
Are you alone?	Sei solo/a? / Lei è solo/a?
May I invite you to a ...?	Vorrei invitarti/la a ...?
bar	un bar
night club	un night(club)
restaurant	un ristorante
theatre	un teatro
cinema	un cinema
dance	un ballo
drink	prendere qualche cosa

meal / lunch / dinner	mangiare / pranzo / cena
dance	ballare
show	uno spettacolo
play	un'opera teatrale
musical	un musical
comedy	una commedia
concert	un concerto

Useful verbs

to introduce	presentare
to arrange a meeting	fissare un appuntamento
to book a table	riservare un tavolo
to go to the cinema	andare al cinema
to go to the theatre	andare al teatro
to go out	uscire
to go to a night club	andare in un night (club)
to watch a video	vedere un video

Useful phrases

How are you?	Come stai? / Come sta?
How's it going?	Come va?
Very well thank you	Molto bene, grazie
Have a nice day / weekend	Buona giornata / Buon fine settimana
See you soon	A presto
See you later	A più tardi
See you next time	Alla prossima volta
See you tomorrow	A domani
What would you like to do?	Che ti/le piacerebbe fare?
Where would you like to go?	Dove ti/le piacerebbe andare?
When shall we meet?	A che ora ci ritroviamo?
I will pick you up	Passerò a prenderti/la
Excuse me	Scusa (familiar) / Scusi (formal)
Pardon?	Come? / Scusi? / Prego?
I don't understand	Non capisco
Can you speak more slowly	Parla / parli più lentamente
I apologize / I'm sorry	Mi scusi
I beg your pardon	Prego
I didn't mean it	Non avevo l'intenzione di farlo

Forgive me	Scusami (familiar) / mi scusi (formal)
… it was my fault	è stata colpa mia
It was your fault	È stata colpa tua / sua
Thank you very much	Grazie mille
I enjoyed it very much	Mi è piaciuto molto
I had a lovely time	Mi sono divertito molto
We must do it again sometime	Dobbiamo farlo un'altra volta
I will see you tomorrow / later	Ci vediamo domani / più tardi
I would like to see you again	Mi piacerebbe vederti/la un'altra volta
It's a pleasure	è un piacere / prego!
Have a good time!	Buon divertimento!
Have a safe journey	Buon viaggio
Good luck	Buona fortuna!
All the best	Che tutto vada per il meglio!
Happy birthday	Buon compleanno
Merry Christmas	Buon Natale
Congratulations	Congratulazioni
Happy New Year	Buon Anno
Anyway …	In ogni caso … / comunque …
Er …	Ehm …
Uhm …	Mmm …
Ah!	Aaa!
etc. (etcetera)	ecc. (eccetera)
i.e. (that is)	cioè
e.g. (for example)	ad es. (ad esempio)
a.s.a.p (as soon as possible)	prima possibile

How to say *you*

Dare del tu / dare del lei

ℹ️ In Italian, you need to decide how to address the person you are speaking to. The informal **tu** is used for family, close friends and acquaintances, and in most cases anyone of an age and status similar to yours, even if you don't yet know them. The formal **Lei** is used for strangers and those older than you or senior in status. In Italy this is more relaxed than it used to be, but if in doubt when meeting someone for the first time, use **Lei** until invited to use **tu**. Your new acquaintance will probably use an expression such as **'mi potresti dare del tu'** to invite you to be informal. Just to remind you, where both **tu** and **Lei** forms of a verb are given, the **tu** form is first.

1.2 Where are you from?

Core vocabulary

Where do you come from? *Da dove vieni? / Da dove viene?*

I come from …		Sono di/Vengo da	
I am …		Sono …	
I speak …		Parlo …	

Austria	Austria	*Austrian*	austriaco/a
Belgium	Belgio	*Belgian*	belga
Ireland	Irlanda	*Irish*	irlandese
England	Inghilterra	*English*	inglese
France	Francia	*French*	francese
Germany	Germania	*German*	tedesco/a
Greece	Grecia	*Greek*	greco/a
Italy	Italia	*Italian*	italiano/a
Scotland	Scozia	*Scottish*	scozzese
Spain	Spagna	*Spanish*	spagnolo/a
Switzerland	Svizzera	*Swiss*	svizzero/a
Wales	Galles	*Welsh*	gallese

In each case the masculine form of the nationality is the name of the language, except in the case of countries which do not have their own language.

Africa	Africa	*African*	africano/a
America	America	*American*	americano/a
Australia	Australia	*Australian*	australiano/a
Croatia	Croazia	*Croatian*	croato/a
Denmark	Danimarca	*Danish*	danese
Finland	Finlandia	*Finnish*	finlandese
Hungary	Ungheria	*Hungarian*	ungherese
India	indiano	*India*	indiano/a
New Zealand	Nuova Zelanda	*New Zealander*	neozelandese
Norway	Norvegia	*Norwegian*	norvegese
Poland	Polonia	*Polish*	polacco/a
Russia	Russia	*Russian*	russo/a
Sweden	Svezia	*Swedish*	svedese

There are a number of British place names for which there is an Italian version:

the United Kingdom	Il Regno Unito
Great Britain	Gran Bretagna
England	Inghilterra
Wales	Galles
Scotland	Scozia
Northern Ireland	Irlanda del Nord
London	Londra
Edinburgh	Edimburgo
Thames	Il Tamigi
Cornwall	Cornovaglia

There are also a number of foreign cities which have an Italian version:

Athens	Atene
Belgrade	Belgrado
Moscow	Mosca
Paris	Parigi
Berlin	Berlino
Stockholm	Stoccolma
Hamburg	Amburgo
the Hague	L'Aia

Useful phrases

Do you speak English?	Parli inglese? / Parla inglese?
What languages do you speak?	Che lingue parli / parla?
What nationality are you?	Di che nazionalità sei / è?
Where were you born?	Dove sei nato/a? / Dov'è nato/a?
I was born in …	Sono nato/a in …
I live …	Vivo / Abito …
in the north / south / east / west	nel nord / nel sud / nell'est / nell'ovest
middle	nel centro
near the sea	vicino al mare
on the coast	sulla costa
in the mountains	in montagna
in the city	in città
in a village	in un paese / villaggio
in the suburbs	in periferia
in the country	in campagna

Useful verbs

to live	vivere/ abitare	I live …	vivo/ abito
to speak	parlare	I speak	parlo
to be born	nascere	I was born in …	sono nato/a in …

1.3 Personal appearance

Core vocabulary

What are you like?	Come sei / Com'è?
I am a …	Sono un(a) …
What does he/she look like?	Com'è lui/lei?
He / She is a …	È …
man	un uomo
woman	una donna
girl	una ragazza
boy	un ragazzo
teenager	un/un'adolescente
child	un bambino / una bambina
baby	un bambino piccolo / una bambina piccola

Use the following grid to help you to build up what you need to be able to say to describe yourself and someone you know well.

I am	sono	quite	tall
		abbastanza	alto/a
Are you …?	È / Sei …?	very	short/small
		molto	piccolo/a
			basso/a
He/she is	Lui/lei è	average	
			di statura media

I have	Ho	long blonde hair
		capelli biondi lunghi
He has	(Lui) ha	short brown hair
		capelli castani corti
She has	(Lei) ha	medium length dark hair
		capelli scuri di media lunghezza
I have	ho	blue/brown eyes
		occhi azzurri/castani

attractive	attraente	*unattractive*	poco attraente
fashionable	di moda	*unfashionable*	fuori moda
fit	in forma	*unfit*	non in forma
good looking	bello/a	*ugly*	brutto/a
neat	ordinato/a	*untidy*	disordinato/a
smart	elegante	*scruffy*	trasandato/a
ordinary	normale	*different*	diverso
tall	alto/a	*short*	basso/a
underweight	sottopeso/a	*overweight*	sovrappeso/a
well built	ben fatto	*weak/skinny*	debole / magro/a
anorexic	anoressico/a	*obese*	obeso/a
right-handed	che usa la mano destra	*left-handed*	mancino/a
short-sighted	miope	*long sighted*	presbite
agoraphobic	agorafobo/a	*claustrophobic*	claustrofobico/a

Here are some of the more colloquial words used in Italy to describe people:

butch (man)	macho
butch (woman)	mascolina
getting on a bit	di una certa età
teenager	l'adolescente
brat, kid, youngster	moccioso/a
bird (girl)	la tipa/bambola
cool, handsome	figo

Useful phrases

How much do you weigh?	Quanto pesi? / Quanto pesa?
I weigh 75 kg	Peso 75 kg
How tall are you?	Quanto sei alto/a?/ Quanto è alto/a?
I am 1.59 m	Sono alto/a 1.59 m

Useful verbs

to look like someone	rassomigliare a qualcuno
to put on weight	ingrassare
to lose weight	dimagrire
to get fit	mettersi in forma

1.4 What sort of person are you?

Core vocabulary

character and feelings *temperamento e sentimenti*

ℹ️ If you are describing somebody, you need to decide whether you are talking about their character, in which case you need an expression with the verb **essere** like those in the following chart, or you are talking about how they are or how they feel, in which case you need an expression with the verb **stare** (see p. 17). Remember that the adjectives have to agree with the noun.

I am	sono	*shy / talkative*	timido / loquace
are you?	sei / è?	*happy / unhappy*	felice / infelice
he is	(lui) è	*friendly / unfriendly*	amichevole / poco amichevole
she is	(lei) è	*nice / nasty*	simpatico / antipatico

I am	sono	*happy / sad*	contento / triste
are you?	sei / è?	*awake / tired*	sveglio / stanco
he is	(lui) è	*smart / scruffy*	elegante / trasandato
she is	(lei) è	*in a good / bad mood*	di buon / cattivo umore

Here are some extra adjectives you could use to describe people.

good	buono	*bad*	cattivo
hard-working	diligente	*lazy*	pigro
interesting	interessante	*boring*	noioso
quiet	tranquillo	*loud*	rumoroso
strong	forte	*weak*	debole
capable	capace	*useless*	incapace
confident	sicuro di sé	*nervous*	nervoso/ansioso
generous	generoso	*mean*	tirchio
helpful	disponibile	*unhelpful*	poco disponibile
odd	strano	*normal*	normale
polite	educato	*rude*	maleducato
practical	pratico	*impractical*	poco pratico
reliable	affidabile	*unreliable*	inaffidabile
relaxed	rilassato	*up-tight*	teso
sensible	sensato	*stupid*	stupido
sensitive	sensibile	*unfeeling*	insensibile
serious	serio	*frivolous*	frivolo

sincere	sincero	*insincere*	insincero
strong-willed	prepotente	*weak*	debole
well-behaved	che si comporta bene	*badly behaved*	che si comporta male
up-to-date	di moda	*out-of-date*	fuori moda

the five senses *i cinque sensi*

sight	la vista	*to see*	vedere	*I see*	vedo
hearing	l'udito	*to hear*	sentire	*I hear*	sento
taste	il gusto	*to taste*	assaggiare	*I taste*	assaggio
smell	l'olfatto	*to smell*	sentire odore di	*I smell*	sento odore di
touch	il tatto	*to touch*	toccare	*I touch*	tocco

Useful phrases

He / she has ...	(Lui / lei) ha ...
a sense of humour	il senso dell'umorismo
plenty of will power	molta forza di volontà
a kind heart	bontà di cuore
a weakness for ...	un debole per ...
a good imagination	una buon'immaginazione

Useful verbs

to get bored	annoiarsi
I am getting bored	mi annoio
to be interested in something	interessarsi a/di
I am interested	mi interesso a/di
to be worried about something	preoccuparsi di
I am worried	mi preoccupo di

Other useful adjectives

angry	arrabbiato
annoyed	seccato
kind	gentile
unkind	poco gentile
laid back	rilassato
dynamic	dinamico

False friends

You may have noticed a couple of **falsi amici** *false friends* in this area. This table should help you:

English	Italian
sensitive	sensibile
sensible	sensato
nice, kind	simpatico
sympathetic	comprensivo

i Lots of expressions we use in English like *to be hot*, *cold*, *hungry*, *thirsty* and so on are expressed in Italian using the verb **avere** as in the following table:

to be hot	avere caldo	*I am hot*	ho caldo
to be cold	avere freddo	*he is cold*	ha freddo
to be hungry	avere fame	*we are hungry*	abbiamo fame
to be thirsty	avere sete	*you are thirsty*	hai sete
to be tired	avere sonno	*they are tired*	hanno sonno
to be in a hurry	avere fretta	*she is in a hurry*	ha fretta
to be afraid	avere paura	*they are afraid*	hanno paura

1.5 My things

Core vocabulary

things	le cose
bag	la borsa
briefcase	la cartella
cheque book	il libretto degli assegni
credit cards	le carte di credito
diary	l'agenda
driving licence	la patente di guida
glasses / sunglasses	gli occhiali (da sole)
keys	le chiavi
note book	il taccuino / il bloc-notes
passport	il passaporto
pen	la penna
purse	il portamonete
wallet	il portafoglio
watch	l'orologio

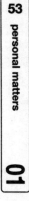

i The words for *my/your/his/her/our/their* follow this pattern:

my	il mio, la mia
	i miei, le mie
your (familiar)	il tuo, la tua
	i tuoi, le tue
his, her,	il suo, la sua
your (formal)	i suoi, le sue
our	il nostro, la nostra
	i nostri, le nostre
your	il vostro, la vostra
	i vostri, le vostre
their,	il loro, la loro
your (formal)	i loro, le loro

on my desk *sulla mia scrivania*

computer	il computer
hard drive	l'hard disk
mobile	il telefonino / cellulare
mouse	il mouse
laptop	il laptop
palm-top	il palmare
PC	il PC
phone	il telefono
printer	la stampante
scanner	lo scanner

at home *a casa*

DVD player	il lettore DVD
CD player	il lettore CD
discs	i dischi
camera	la macchina fotografica
video camera	la videocamera
digital camera	la macchina fotografica digitale
film	la pellicola
roll of film	il rullino
photos	le foto

my friends *i miei amici / le mie amiche*

girl friend(s)	le mie amiche
boy friend(s)	i miei amici
girlfriend	la mia ragazza
boyfriend	il mio ragazzo
colleagues	i miei colleghi

Here are a few expressions used in colloquial Italian:

my bike	la mia bici
my TV	la mia tivù
my better half	la mia dolce metà
my kids	i miei bambini

Useful phrases

Have you got a ... ?	Hai / Ha un/uno/una/un'...?
I have lost my ...	Ho perso (perduto) il mio / la mia / i miei / le mie ...
I can't find my ...	Non trovo il mio / la mia / i miei / le mie...
Have you seen my ...?	Hai / Ha visto il mio / la mia / i miei / le mie...?

Useful verbs

to lose / mislay	perdere
to find	trovare
to forget	dimenticare

1.6 I think, I feel

Core vocabulary

to like	piacere	*I like*	mi piace
to love	amare	*I love*	amo
to prefer	preferire	*I prefer*	preferisco
to dislike	non piacere	*I dislike*	non mi piace
to hate	odiare	*I hate*	odio

i The verb **piacere** is used to express the idea of liking, but has to do it back-to-front, because it really means '*to please*'! So what you really say is '*this car pleases me*' '**mi piace questa macchina**'. Study the following table and learn the examples to help you remember how to use this expression. Note how the person word changes, and that only two verb endings are used, to match the thing or things liked, not the person liking. It really is back to front!

	singular things	plural things
I like	mi piace	mi piacciono
you like (familiar sing.)	ti piace	ti piacciono
he / she likes	gli / le piace	gli / le piacciono
you like (formal sing.)	Le piace	Le piacciono
we like	ci piace	ci piacciono
you like (familiar pl.)	vi piace	vi piaccciono
they like	gli piace	gli piacciono
you like (formal pl.)	piace a Loro	piacciono a Loro

I like wine	mi piace il vino
I like tomatoes	mi piacciono i pomodori
you like beer	ti piace la birra
you like oranges	ti piacciono le arance
he likes football	gli piace il calcio
she likes sweets	le piacciono le caramelle
we like Italy	ci piace l'Italia
we like Italian people	ci piacciono gli italiani
you like working	vi piace lavorare
you like public holidays	vi piacciono i giorni festivi
they like travelling	gli piace viaggiare
they like holidays	gli piacciono le vacanze

to believe	credere	I believe	credo
to think	pensare	I think	penso
to feel	sentirsi	I feel	mi sento
to worry	preoccuparsi	I worry	mi preoccupo
to advise	consigliare	I advise	consiglio
to encourage	incoraggiare	I encourage	incoraggio
to exaggerate	esagerare	I am exaggerating	esagero
to joke	scherzare	I am joking	sto scherzando
to lie	dire bugie	I am lying	dico bugie
to promise	promettere	I promise	prometto

i Note that **credere** and **pensare** need a subjunctive verb after them when used in the negative if there is a subordinate clause (See p.23).)

non credo che ci sia	I don't believe he is there
non penso che abbiano paura	I don't think they are afraid

Useful verbs

to be disappointed	essere deluso
to be relieved	essere sollevato
to be depressed	essere depresso
to be elated	essere euforico
to be stressed	essere stressato
to be relaxed	essere rilassato
to be discouraged	essere scoraggiato
to be encouraged	essere incoraggiato
to be embarrassed	essere imbarazzato
to be at ease	essere/sentirsi a proprio agio
to be nervous	essere nervoso
to be confident	essere sicuro
to be worried	essere preoccupato
to be reassured	essere rassicurato
to be sad	essere triste
to be happy	essere contento
to be ashamed	vergognarsi
to be proud	essere orgoglioso/fiero
to be unfortunate	essere sfortunato
to be fortunate	essere fortunato

Verbs which are used with another verb

to want to	volere	*I want to go*	voglio andare
to be able to	potere	*I can go in*	posso entrare
to have to	dovere	*I must leave*	devo partire
to need to	avere bisogno di	*I need to go out*	ho bisogno di uscire
ought to / should	dovere	*I should stay at home*	dovrei rimanere a casa

Useful phrases

There are a number of impersonal expressions in Italian which consist of è + an adjective + an infinitive.

it's necessary	è necessario arrivare alle dieci	*it's necessary to arrive at ten*
it's vital	è essenziale farlo	*it's vital to do it*
it's obligatory	è obbligatorio pagare la bolletta	*it's obligatory to pay the bill*

it's possible	è possibile uscire	it's possible to go out
it's impossible	è impossibile sapere	it's impossible to know
it's dangerous	è pericoloso nuotare qui	it's dangerous to swim here
it's horrible	è orribile vederlo così	it's horrible to see him like this
it's prohibited	è vietato attaccare manifesti	it's prohibited to put up posters

What is it like?

acceptable	accettabile	comfortable	comodo
considerable	considerevole	probable	probabile
possible	possibile	preferable	preferibile
remarkable	straordinario	responsible	responsabile
tolerable	sopportabile		

i Most words which end in -able or -ible in English are similar in Italian, adding an extra -i before -le, but in Italian remember to pronounce the vowels clearly and to stress the a of -abile or the i of -ibile.

1.7 Expressing an opinion

to believe	credere	I believe	credo
to consider	considerare	I consider	considero
to think	pensare	I think	penso
to agree / disagree	essere / non essere d'accordo	I agree / disagree	sono / non sono d'accordo
to argue (maintain)	sostenere	I argue	discuto
to argue (debate)	discutere	I argue	dibatto
to ask	domandare	I ask	domando
to dispute	contestare	I dispute	contesto
to question	mettere in dubbio	I question	metto in dubbio
to quote	citare	I quote	cito

to request	chiedere	I request	chiedo
to suggest	suggerire	I suggest	suggerisco
to state	dichiarare	I would like to say	dichiaro
to compare	confrontare	I compare	confronto
to contrast	contrastare	I contrast	contrasto
to differ	dissentire	I differ	dissento
to discuss	discutere	I discuss	discuto
to conclude	concludere	I conclude	concludo

on the one hand	da una parte
on the other hand	d'altra parte
firstly	in primo luogo
secondly	in secondo luogo
finally	alla fine
actually	veramente
basically	fondamentalmente
clearly	chiaramente
consequently	di conseguenza / quindi
fortunately / unfortunately	fortunatamente / purtroppo
generally	generalmente
honestly	francamente
mainly	principalmente / soprattutto
normally	normalmente
obviously	ovviamente
particularly	specialmente
principally	principalmente
really	davvero
usually / unusually	di solito / insolitamente
in my / his / her opinion	secondo me / lui / lei
above all	soprattutto
although	benché
as a result	di conseguenza
as well as	oltre a
however	però / comunque
in some respects	sotto certi aspetti
in spite of	malgrado
instead of	invece di
nevertheless	tuttavia
otherwise	altrimenti
similarly	allo stesso modo
the reason is	è perché
to tell the truth	a dire la verità

I *wish I could agree*	vorrei poter essere d'accordo
I *beg to differ*	mi permetto di non essere d'accordo
I *mean*	voglio dire
I *maintain*	sostengo
for example	per esempio
etc.	eccetera / ecc.
in brief	in breve
the advantages / disadvantages are	i vantaggi / gli svantaggi sono
the pros and cons	i pro e i contro
to conclude	concludere
it is	è
bad / good	cattivo / male / buono / bene
comfortable / uncomfortable	comodo / scomodo
better / worse	migliore / meglio / peggiore / peggio
nice / not very nice	piacevole / spiacevole
too hard / easy	troppo difficile / facile

1.8 I do (I + useful action verbs)

Useful verbs

to *wake up*	svegliarsi	I *wake up*	mi sveglio
to *get up*	alzarsi	I *get up*	mi alzo
to *take a shower*	fare la doccia	I *take a shower*	faccio la doccia
to *get dressed*	vestirsi	I *get dressed*	mi vesto
to *eat*	mangiare	I *eat*	mangio
to *drink*	bere	I *drink*	bevo
to *work*	lavorare	I *work*	lavoro
to *go home*	tornare a casa	I *go home*	torno a casa
to *play*	giocare	I *play*	gioco
to *watch television*	guardare la televisione	I *watch*	guardo la televisione
to *read*	leggere	I *read*	leggo
to *get washed*	lavarsi	I *get washed*	mi lavo
to *go to bed*	andare a letto	I *go to bed*	vado a letto
to *laugh*	ridere	I *laugh*	rido
to *smile*	sorridere	I *smile*	sorrido
to *giggle*	avere la risarella	I *giggle*	ho la risarella

| to sleep | dormire | I sleep | dormo |
| to dream | sognare | I dream | sogno |

coming and going verbs *verbi di movimento*

to walk	camminare	I walk	cammino
to run	correre	I run	corro
to ride	andare a / in	I ride	vado a / in
to drive	guidare	I drive	guido
to arrive	arrivare	I arrive	arrivo
to depart	partire	I depart	parto
to enter	entrare	I enter	entro
to leave	partire	I leave	parto
to come	venire	I come	vengo
to go	andare	I go	vado
to go up	salire	I go up	salgo
to go down	scendere	I go down	scendo
to stay	rimanere	I stay	rimango
to return	tornare	I return	torno

communicating *comunicare*

to speak	parlare
to repeat something	ripetere qualcosa
to talk to someone	parlare con qualcuno
to whisper to someone	bisbigliare a qualcuno
to shout at someone	gridare a qualcuno
to ask a question	fare una domanda
to ask for something	chiedere qualcosa
to respond to a question	rispondere a una domanda
to tell a story	raccontare una storia
to enjoy yourself	divertirsi
to get angry	arrabbiarsi
to have trouble / difficulty	avere difficoltà
to get depressed	deprimersi
to know / meet someone	conoscere / incontrare qualcuno
to know something	sapere qualcosa
to cheat	imbrogliare
to trick	ingannare
to challenge	sfidare
to compliment	complimentarsi con
to neglect	trascurare

1.9 Don't panic!

Useful phrases

Help!	Aiuto!
Listen!	Ascolta! / Ascolti!
Do you understand?	Capisci? / Capisce?
Understood?	Hai capito? / Ha capito?
Can you help me?	Mi puoi / può aiutare?
Do you speak English?	Parli / Parla inglese?
Can you speak more slowly?	Parla / Parli più lentamente!
I didn't catch what you said	Non ho colto quello che hai/ha detto
Please can you find someone who speaks English?	Può trovare qualcuno che parli inglese?
Can you write it down for me please?	Scrivilo / Lo scriva per favore
How do you spell it?	Come si scrive?
Have you got the phone number for ...?	Hai / Ha il numero di telefono ...?
police	della polizia
fire brigade	dei vigili del fuoco
ambulance	dell'ambulanza
doctor	del medico
breakdown services	dei servizi di soccorso stradale
What do I need to dial first?	Quale prefisso devo comporre?
What is the code for ...?	Qual è il prefisso di/per ...?
How do I get an outside line?	Come posso avere una linea esterna?
Danger	Pericolo
Watch out!	Attenzione!
Warning	Avviso
No entry	Vietato l'ingresso

02 family

2.1 My family

Core vocabulary

my family and relatives *la mia famiglia e i miei parenti*

my mother	mia madre
my father	mio padre
my parents	i miei genitori
my sister	mia sorella
my brother	mio fratello
my younger brother	il mio fratello minore
my younger sister	la mia sorella minore
my older brother	il mio fratello maggiore
my older sister	la mia sorella maggiore
my half-brother	il mio fratellastro
my half-sister	la mia sorellastra
twin brother	il mio fratello gemello
twin sister	la mia sorella gemella
my grandmother	mia nonna
my grandfather	mio nonno
my grandparents	i miei nonni
my great-grandparents	i miei bisnonni
my grandson	mio nipote
my granddaughter	mia nipote
my uncle	mio zio
my aunt	mia zia
my cousin (m)	mio cugino
my cousin (f)	mia cugina
my nephew	mio nipote
my niece	mia nipote
my husband	mio marito
my wife	mia moglie
my ex-husband	il mio ex-marito
my ex-wife	la mia ex-moglie
my father-in law	mio suocero
my mother-in-law	mia suocera
my brother-in-law	mio cognato
my sister-in-law	mia cognata
my partner	il mio / la mia partner
my friend	il mio amico / la mia amica
my boyfriend	il mio ragazzo
my girlfriend	la mia ragazza
my godson	il mio figlioccio
my goddaughter	la mia figlioccia

a married couple	una coppia di sposi
widow	la vedova
widower	il vedovo

pet names *vezzeggiativi*

darling	caro/a
darling / sweetheart	tesoro / amore
daddy	papà / babbo
mummy	mamma
grandpa	nonno
grandma, nan	nonna
kiddy	bambino

Useful verbs

to like someone	avere simpatia per qualcuno / piacere*
to flirt	flirtare
to kiss	baciare
to go out with someone	uscire con qualcuno
to get on with someone	andare d'accordo con qualcuno
to have a good time	divertirsi
to have intercourse / sex	avere rapporti sessuali
to get married	sposarsi
to get on each other's nerves	darsi ai nervi
to look after someone	occuparsi di
to quarrel	litigare
to separate	separarsi
to divorce	divorziare

*see pp. 54–55

Useful phrases

May I introduce my ...	Ti presento mio/mia ... / Questo/a è mio/mia ....
Pleased to meet you	Piacere! / Molto lieto!
I am sorry to hear about your separation / divorce / bereavement	Mi dispiace (sapere) che si è separato / che ha divorziato / che è in lutto.
Will you go out with me?	Vuoi / vuole uscire con me?
I am going out with ...	Esco con ...
We are just good friends.	Siamo solo buoni amici.

Tips for remembering words

- Remember that lots of words for family members can be grouped in pairs – **figlio/a, cugino/a** and so on. Try to associate the words with members of your own family – you could draw your own family tree and label it.

- Think of **padre** as being a word we use for a *priest* (*Father* ...) and as being related to our word *paternal*; similarly with **madre** and *maternal*.

2.2 Children

Core vocabulary

baby	il bebé
infant	il bambino piccolo / la bambina piccola
child	il bambino / la bambina
boy	il ragazzo / il bambino
girl	la ragazza / la bambina
twin	il gemello / la gemella
teenager	l'adolescente / il/la teenager
adolescent	l'adolescente
pregnancy	la gravidanza
birth	la nascita / il parto
newborn baby	il neonato / la neonata
nanny	la bambinaia
childminder	la bambinaia
babysitter	il/la babysitter
midwife	l'ostetrica
crèche	l'asilo nido
playschool	l'asilo
baby's bottle	il biberon
teat	la tettarella
dummy	il succhiotto
bib	il bavaglino
babymilk	il latte per bambini
high chair	il seggiolone
nappy	il pannolino
carrycot	la culla portatile
cot	il lettino
pram	la carrozzina
pushchair	il passeggino
toy	il giocattolo

wind	il ruttino
colic	la colica
an only child	figlio unico / figlia unica
an adopted child	un bambino adottivo
an orphan	un orfano
children's playground	il parco giochi
swing	l'altalena
slide	lo scivolo
roundabout	la giostra

i In Italy, 'family festivals' are largely like ours: events such as christenings, birthdays, weddings and funerals are important family events, at which the wider family will gather to celebrate – or commiserate – with relatives. There are special traditions attached to these events, too many to mention here. However, two extra 'special' events are celebrated in Italy:

- Many people still celebrate their onomastico or *saint's day* – the day dedicated to the saint whose name they carry. Thus, a Pietro will celebrate St Peter's day on June 29th, a Michele will celebrate St Michael's day, September 29th (Michaelmas); girls called Maria may celebrate dates such as August 15 and October 12, there being many feast-days devoted to the mother of Jesus.

- Many Italians are Roman Catholics, and celebrate **la Prima Comunione** *the First Communion* of their children, usually in June. You may come across other such religious events: you could ask an Italian friend to explain them, and hopefully you you might understand the answer!

Useful verbs

to be expecting a baby	aspettare un bambino
to breastfeed	allattare (al seno)
to burp	ruttare
to change a nappy	cambiare un pannolino
to cry	piangere
to feed	poppare
to give a bottle	dare il biberon
to rock	far dondolare / cullare
to teethe	mettere i denti
to look after	prendersi cura di
to childmind	sorvegliare un bambino
to babysit	guardare i bambini / fare il/la babysitter

Useful phrases

I *am pregnant*	sono incinta
I'm *on the pill*	prendo la pillola
It's *a boy/girl*	è un maschio / una femmina
sibling rivalry	la rivalità tra fratelli
family planning	la pianificazione familiare
a spoilt child	un bambino viziato
I *need*	ho bisogno di
a cream for a sore bottom	una pomata per irritazione da pannolini
sun cream for children	una crema solare per bambini
shampoo for children	uno shampoo per bambini
something for wind	qualcosa per la flatulenza
for children teething	qualcosa per la dentizione

Word-building

i You will notice that often one word will have another word or words based on it; here are some examples:

child	il bambino	→ la bambinaia	*nanny*
to drink	bere	→ il biberon	*baby's bottle*
chair	sedia	→ seggiolone	*high chair*
to go for a walk	passeggiare	→ il passeggino	*pushchair*

2.3 Anniversaries, marriage and death

Core vocabulary

birthday	il compleanno
engagement	il fidanzamento
marriage	il matrimonio
death	la morte
the wedding	le nozze / il matrimonio
church	la chiesa
town hall	il municipio
engagement ring	l'anello di fidanzamento
wedding invitation	la partecipazione di nozze
wedding day	il giorno delle nozze
wedding dress	l'abito da sposa
wedding ceremony	la cerimonia nuziale
wedding ring	la fede / vera

wedding certificate	il certificato di matrimonio
wedding cake	la torta nuziale
bride	la sposa
bridegroom	lo sposo
bridesmaid	la damigella d'onore
honeymoon	la luna di miele / il viaggio di nozze
married life	la vita matrimoniale / coniugale
separation	la separazione
divorce	il divorzio
silver wedding anniversary	le nozze d'argento
golden wedding anniversary	le nozze d'oro
heterosexual	eterosessuale
homosexual	omosessuale
lesbian	lesbica
death	la morte
funeral	il funerale
corpse	il cadavere
coffin	la bara
cemetery	il cimitero
burial	il seppellimento
cremation	la cremazione
grave	la tomba
death duties	la tassa di successione
death certificate	il certificato di morte
will	il testamento

Useful verbs

to get engaged	fidanzarsi
to get married	sposarsi
to die	morire
to be buried	essere seppellito
to be in mourning	essere in lutto
to kill yourself	suicidarsi

Useful phrases

Congratulations!	Congratulazioni!
Happy birthday	Buon compleanno!
Congratulations on your engagement	Congratulazioni per il tuo fidanzamento
wedding	il tuo matrimonio

anniversary   il tuo anniversario

We *would like to wish you*
every future happiness   Vi auguriamo ogni felicità per il futuro

We *would like to send you*
our best wishes   Vi inviamo i migliori auguri

I *would like to convey*
my condolences   Le / Vi porgo le mie più sentite condoglianze

I *am very sorry to learn of*
your sad loss   Ho appreso con immenso dolore della scomparsa del suo caro

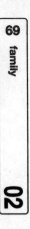

03

work

3.1 Job titles

After **sono, sei, è** etc., you don't need **un/una** in front of jobs and professions.

Core vocabulary

accountant	il/la contabile, il ragioniere/ la ragioniera
actor/actress	l'attore / l'attrice
architect	l'architetto
builder	il muratore
businessman	l'uomo d'affari, l'imprenditore
civil servant	l'impiegato statale
dentist	il/la dentista
doctor	il medico, il dottore / la dottoressa
driver	l'autista
electrician	l'elettricista
engineer	l'ingegnere
farmer	l'agricoltore
farm worker	il/la bracciante
fireman	il pompiere, il vigile del fuoco
hairdresser	il parrucchiere / la parrucchiera
journalist	il/la giornalista
lawyer	l'avvocato / l'avvocatessa
lecturer / professor	il professore / la professoressa
mechanic	il meccanico
musician	il/la musicista
nurse	l'infermiere / l'infermiera
plumber	l'idraulico
policeman	il poliziotto, l'agente di polizia
policewoman	la donna poliziotto
postman	il postino / la postina
receptionist	il/la receptionist
scientist	lo scienziato / la scienziata
secretary	il segretario / la segretaria
shop assistant	il commesso / la commessa
shopkeeper	il/la negoziante
student	lo studente / la studentessa
waiter/waitress	il cameriere / la cameriera
worker	l'operaio / l'operaia
unemployed	disoccupato / senza lavoro
retired	pensionato / in pensione

the staff *il personale*

chairman	il presidente
chief executive	il direttore generale
managing director	l'amministratore delegato
director	il dirigente / direttore
company secretary	il segretario generale
departmental head	il capo di dipartimento
accountant	il ragioniere / contabile
manager	il dirigente / direttore
business consultant	il consulente commerciale
personal assistant	il segretario / la segretaria particolare
employer	il datore di lavoro
employee	il/la dipendente
sales representative	il/la rappresentante di commercio
computer operator	il/la terminalista
computer programmer	il programmatore / la programmatrice di computer
secretary	il segretario / la segretaria
caretaker	il/la custode, il bidello / la bidella
cleaner	l'addetto/a alle pulizie
businessman	l'uomo d'affari
businesswoman	l'imprenditrice
trainee	l'apprendista

areas of work *settori di lavoro*

agriculture	l'agricoltura
banking	il settore bancario
building trade	l'industria edilizia
catering	il catering
civil service	l'amministrazione pubblica
commerce	il commercio
finance	il settore finanziario
the hotel industry	il settore alberghiero
insurance	l'assicurazione
leisure services	i servizi ricreativi
manufacturing	le industrie manifatturiere
medicine	la medicina
the media	i mass media
the public services	i servizi pubblici
purchasing	il settore acquisti
retail	il commercio al dettaglio
service industry	il settore terziario

show business	il mondo dello spettacolo
textiles	l'industria tessile
tourism	il turismo
transport	il trasporto
wholesale	il commercio all'ingrosso

Useful verbs

to work / earn my living	lavorare / guadagnarmi da vivere
to be out of work	essere disoccupato
to buy / sell	comprare / vendere
to import / export	importare / esportare
to manage	dirigere
to manufacture	fabbricare

Useful phrases

I'd like to work as / in …	mi piacerebbe lavorare come / in
I work as / in	lavoro come / in
I used to work as / in	lavoravo come / in

Word building

work	il lavoro
to work	lavorare
worker (m)	il lavoratore
worker (f)	la lavoratrice
employment	l'occupazione / l'impiego
unemployment	la disoccupazione
employed	impiegato
unemployed	disoccupato

3.2 Where do you work?

Core vocabulary

I work in a/an …	lavoro in …
bank	una banca
factory	una fabbrica
farm	una fattoria
garage	un'autofficina
hospital	un ospedale
hotel	un albergo

mine	una miniera
office	un ufficio
post office	un ufficio postale
railways	ferrovia
restaurant	un ristorante
school	una scuola
service station	una stazione di servizio
shopping centre	un centro commerciale
studio	uno studio
town hall	un municipio
workshop	un'officina

the company	la compagnia / società
headquarters	la sede centrale
subsidiary	la filiale
firm	l'azienda / ditta
factory	la fabbrica
limited company	la società a responsabilità limitata

I work in a shop	lavoro in un negozio
... on a building site	... in cantiere di costruzione
... in a sports centre	... in un centro sportivo
... outdoors	... fuori / all'aria aperta
... indoors	... al coperto

3.3 The office

Core vocabulary

the premises	il locale
boardroom	la sala del consiglio
canteen	la mensa
meeting room	la sala delle riunioni
reception	la reception
entrance	l'ingresso / l'entrata
exit	l'uscita
security code	il codice di sicurezza
pass	il lasciapassare / permesso
I work in the ... department	lavoro nella sezione / nel reparto ...
accounts	contabilità
advertising	pubblicità
administration	amministrazione
after-sales	servizio assistenza clienti

catering	catering
distribution	distribuzione
export	esportazione
import	importazione
facilities management	gestione di servizi
information technology	informatica
insurance	assicurazione
manufacturing	fabbricazione
marketing	marketing
personnel / human resources	personale / risorse umane
property	proprietà
purchasing	acquisti
sales	vendite
legal department	il reparto legale
technical department	il reparto tecnico

Useful verbs

to buy	comprare	compro
to manage	dirigere	dirigo
to manufacture	fabbricare	fabbrico
to research	fare ricerca	faccio ricerca
to sell	vendere	vendo
to study	studiare	studio
to travel	viaggiare	viaggio
to work	lavorare	lavoro

Useful phrases

Where do you work?	Dove lavori tu / lavora lei?
Which department do you work in?	In quale reparto lavori / lavora lei?
Our head office is based in …	La nostra sede centrale è basata a …
Please sit down!	Siediti / Si sieda per favore!
Can I get you a coffee?	Posso portarti / portarle un caffè?
Would you like to meet …?	Ti / Le piacerebbe fare la conoscenza di …?

Take care with the few words which are not quite what they appear to be:

il centralino	switchboard
l'interno	extension
l'officina	garage (for repairs and service)

3.4 Conditions of employment

Core vocabulary

working conditions	le condizioni di lavoro
the working day	la giornata lavorativa
the working week	la settimana lavorativa
holidays	le vacanze
annual holiday	le vacanze annuali
national holidays	le feste nazionali
pay / salary	il salario / lo stipendio
income	il reddito
income tax	l'imposta sul reddito
VAT	l'imposta sul valore aggiunto / IVA
applicant	il candidato / la candidata
application	la domanda
application form	il modulo di domanda
CV	il curriculum vitae
contract	il contratto
job interview	il colloquio di lavoro
full-time job	il lavoro a tempo pieno
part-time job	il lavoro part-time
office hours	l'orario d'ufficio
overtime	il lavoro straordinario
flexitime	l'orario flessibile
coffee break	la pausa per il caffè
lunch-time	l'ora di pranzo
meeting	la riunione
leave	il congedo
sick leave	il congedo per malattia
sick note	il certificato di malattia
compassionate leave	il congedo per motivi di famiglia
dismissal	il congedo / licenziamento
redundancy	il licenziamento
union	il sindacato
union meeting	la riunione sindacale
strike	lo sciopero
demand	la rivendicazione
bankruptcy	il fallimento / la bancarotta
lay-off	il licenziamento
standard of living	il tenore di vita

unemployment rate	il tasso di disoccupazione
legal minimum wage	il salario minimo legale

Useful verbs

to be behind with one's work	essere indietro con il lavoro
to catch up with work	mettersi in pari col lavoro
to be ahead	essere in anticipo
to have a deadline	avere una scadenza da rispettare
to be overworked	lavorare troppo
to be stressed	essere stressato

Useful phrases

It is stressful / stimulating	È stressante / stimolante
He is very efficient	Lui è molto efficiente
organized / disorganized	... organizzato / disorganizzato
hard working / lazy	... un gran lavoratore / un pigrone

Word building

There is often a part of the word which can give you a clue to its meaning or help you to remember it.

il direttore	*manager*
il dirigente	*executive*
dirigere	*to manage*
la direzione	*management*

3.5 Writing a letter

- Always write your name/address on the back of the envelope, after the word **mittente** *sender*.
- Only write your town/city and the date at the top right of your letter.

starting an informal letter

Dear Dad / brother / son / grandad	Caro papà / fratello / figlio / nonno
Dear Uncle David	Caro zio Davide
Dear Mum / sister / daughter / grandma	Cara mamma / sorella / figlia / nonna
Dear Aunt Anna	Cara zia Anna

| Dear Giuseppe / Michele / Sergio | Caro Giuseppe / Michele / Sergio |
| Dear friend | Caro amico / Cara amica |

ending an informal letter

Love	Cari saluti
Write soon	Scrivi presto
Give my regards to your father / parents	Salutami tuo padre / i tuoi genitori
Give a kiss to your little brother	Da' un bacio al tuo fratellino
A kiss / hug (= love from ...)	Un bacio / abbraccio (da ...)

starting a formal letter

Dear Mr Paolo / Mr Borletti	Caro signor Paolo / signor Borletti
Dear Mrs Luisa / Miss Morini	Cara signora Luisa / signorina Morini
Dear Sir / Madam	Gentile Signore / Signora
Dear ... (very formal)	Egregio/a ...

ending a formal letter

| Best wishes | Cordiali saluti |
| Yours sincerely (very formal) | Distinti saluti |

3.6 Using the telephone

Core vocabulary

telephone	il telefono
receiver	il ricevitore
extension	l'interno
mobile	il telefonino
telephone number	il numero di telefono
directory	l'elenco (telefonico)
local call	la telefonata urbana
long distance call	la telefonata interurbana
international call	la telefonata internazionale
to phone	telefonare
to call	chiamare
to call back	richiamare
to divert a call	trasferire una chiamata
to put someone through	mettere qualcuno in comunicazione con
to look up a number	cercare un numero

Useful phrases

Hello!	Pronto!
Could I speak to …?	Vorrei parlare con/a …
Can I have extension … please?	Mi dia interno numero … per favore.
Can I have someone who deals with …?	Vorrei parlare con chi si occupa di …
Who is calling?	Chi parla?
Can you tell me what it is about?	Mi può dire di che si tratta?
Who would you like to speak to?	Con chi vuole parlare?
Speaking!	Sono io!
Can you wait a moment?	Può aspettare un attimo?
I am putting you through	Le passo … / La metto in comunicazione
The line is engaged / busy	La linea è occupata
The line is free	La linea è libera
Do you want to hold?	Vuole attendere in linea?
Would you like to leave a message?	Vuole lasciare un messaggio?
Can I take your name and number?	Mi dia il suo nome e il suo numero
I haven't got a signal	Non c'è ricezione
My battery is running low	La mia batteria si sta scaricando / è esaurita
Can you ring back?	Mi può richiamare?
Can you text me?	Mi può spedire un messaggio SMS
Hello – this is …. call me when you can	Pronto – sono … Mi richiami quando può
This is … I'm calling to say I can't go today	Sono … Chiamo per dire che oggi non posso andare
Tell your brother not to come, as there won't be a match	Dica a suo fratello di non venire, che non ci sarà una partita
I'm afraid we can't reserve the room you want	Mi scusi, ma non possiamo riservare la camera che lei desidera

3.7 Using the computer

Core vocabulary

computer	il computer
keyboard	la tastiera
mouse	il mouse
microphone	il microfono
speakers	gli altoparlanti
hard drive	l'hard disc / il disco rigido
screen	lo schermo
laptop	il laptop
printer	la stampante
scanner	lo scanner / il lettore
e-mail	la posta elettronica
world-wide web	il Web
net	la rete
code	il codice
password	la parola d'ordine
programme	il programma
modem	il modem
connector	il connettore
battery	la pila / batteria
phone jack	il jack del telefono

on the screen *sullo schermo*

file	file / archivio
edit	editare
view	vedere / visualizzare
insert	inserire / digitare
format	formato
to format	formattare
font	il carattere
tools	utensili
table	tabella
window	finestra
work	lavoro
help	aiuto

Useful verbs

switch on	accendere
type in	inserire / digitare
log on	aprire una sessione
log off	terminare una sessione

save	salvare
go on line	entrare in linea / on line
send an e-mail	spedire un'e-mail / un messaggio elettronico
receive mail	ricevere un'e-mail / un messaggio elettronico
download a file	trasferire un archivio / file
recharge the battery	ricaricare la pila / batteria

Useful phrases

Have you got a …	Ha un(a) …?
My computer isn't working…	Il mio computer non funziona
Is there any one who can help me?	C'è qualcuno che mi possa aiutare?

04

education

4.1 Primary and secondary education

i School attendance is compulsory in Italy from the age of 6 to 14.

Core vocabulary

headteacher (primary school)	il direttore / la direttrice
headteacher (secondary school)	il/la preside
deputy head (primary school)	il vice-direttore / la vice-direttrice
deputy head (secondary school)	il/la vice-preside
primary teacher	l'insegnante, il maestro / la maestra
secondary teacher	il professore / la professoressa
pupil	l'allievo/a
school secretary	il segretario / la segretaria
school nurse	l'infermiere / l'infermiera di scuola
school caretaker / janitor	il bidello / la bidella
lesson	la lezione
break	l'intervallo
lunch time	l'ora di pranzo
the bell	il campanello
the end of lessons	la fine delle lezioni
term	il trimestre
half term	le vacanze di metà trimestre
holidays	le vacanze
the timetable	l'orario

school subjects *le materie*

Art	il disegno
Biology	la biologia
Chemistry	la chimica
Civics	l'educazione civica
English	l'inglese
French	il francese
History	la storia
Geography	la geografia
German	il tedesco
Information technology	l'informatica
Italian	l'italiano
Maths	la matematica
Music	la musica
P.E.	l'educazione fisica

Physics	la fisica
Science	le scienze
Spanish	lo spagnolo
Technology	la tecnologia

the building *l'edificio*

classroom	la classe / l'aula
corridor	il corridoio
science lab	il laboratorio di scienze
gym	la palestra
games room	la sala giochi
sports hall	la palestra per gli sport di squadra
sports centre	il centro sportivo
music room	l'aula di musica
library	la biblioteca
computer room	l'aula d'informatica
cloakroom	il guardaroba
changing rooms	lo spogliatoio
toilets	i gabinetti

in the classroom *nell'aula*

desk	la cattedra / il banco
blackboard	la lavagna
projector	il proiettore
computer	il computer
white board	la lavagna bianca
interactive white-board	la lavagna bianca interattiva
overhead projector	la lavagna luminosa
book	il libro
exercise book	il quaderno
pencil case	l'astuccio per matite
pen	la penna
biro/ballpoint	la biro / la penna a sfera
pencil	la matita
eraser	la gomma da cancellare
board-rubber	il cancellino
calculator	la calcolatrice
protractor	il goniometro
ruler	la riga / il righello
report	la pagella
school bag	la cartella
sports kit	la tenuta da sport

Useful verbs

to read	leggere
to speak / talk	parlare
to listen	ascoltare
to discuss	discutere
to write	scrivere
to copy	copiare
to take notes	prendere appunti
to be quiet	stare zitto

Useful phrases

to do your homework	fare i compiti
to get a good mark	avere un buon voto
to sit an exam	dare un esame
to pass a test	passare un esame/compito in classe
to fail a test	essere bocciato in un esame/ compito
to re-sit	ripresentarsi a
school hours	l'orario scolastico
progress test	la prova di progresso
final examination	l'esame finale
continuous assessment	la valutazione continua

 Italian school students who fail their end of year exams have to spend much of the summer doing revision lessons to prepare to re-take exams in September **essere rimandato a settembre**; if they fail these exams, they have to repeat the whole year **ripetere l'anno scolastico**, and may even do so two or three times over.

4.2 Further and higher education

Core vocabulary

college	l'istituto superiore
technical college	l'istituto tecnico
university	l'università
faculty	la facoltà
class	la classe
lecture	la lezione / conferenza
seminar / tutorial	il seminario

professor	il docente
full professor	professore ordinario
senior lecturer	professore associato
student	lo studente
research student	lo studente che fa della ricerca
graduate	il laureato
undergraduate	lo studente universitario
apprentice	l'apprendista
trainee	il tirocinante
examination	l'esame
curriculum	il programma
level	il livello
mark / grade	il voto
research	la ricerca
candidate	il candidato
open / competitive examination	il concorso
a paper (research paper)	la relazione
a report	il rapporto
a dissertation	la dissertazione
a thesis	la tesi

Note the false friends:

a research paper (as well as *a relationship*)	una relazione
mark / grade (as well as *a vote*)	un voto
secondary teacher (as well as *a university professor*)	il professore

Useful verbs

to correct	correggere
to discuss	discutere
to explain	spiegare
to learn	imparare
to qualify	abilitarsi
to register/enrol	iscriversi
to study	studiare
to teach	insegnare
to translate	tradurre
to understand	capire
to do research	fare ricerche
to graduate	laurearsi

Useful phrases

to *present a paper*	leggere una relazione
to *do a sandwich course*	fare un corso che alterna lo studio al lavoro
to *study part-time*	studiare part time
to *attend evening class*	seguire un corso serale
to *do work experience*	fare pratica nel mondo del del lavoro

05

at home

5.1 The house

Core vocabulary

house / home	la casa
apartment / flat	l'appartamento
studio	il monolocale
block of flats	il palazzo
building	l'edificio
floor / storey	il piano
ground floor	il pianterreno
first floor	il primo piano
second floor	il secondo piano
basement	il seminterrato
attic	la mansarda
stairs	la scala
lift	l'ascensore
garage	il garage
cellar	la cantina
cottage	la villetta / il cottage
farm	la fattoria
chalet / villa	la villa
council flat	la casa popolare
semi-detached house	la casa bifamiliare
terraced house	la casetta a schiera
central heating	il riscaldamento
double glazing	il doppiovetro
gas	il gas
electricity	l'elettricità
oil	la nafta
water	l'acqua
services	i servizi pubblici
telephone	il telefono
mains sewerage	la rete fognaria
septic tank	la fossa settica
sound proofing	l'insonorizzazione
insulation	l'isolamento termico
shutters	le imposte
Venetian blinds	le veneziane
burglar alarm	l'antifurto
outside	fuori
balcony	il balcone
roof	il tetto

slates	le tegole
terrace	la terrazza
conservatory	la serra
garden	il giardino
gate	il cancello / il portone
path	il sentiero
lawn	il prato all'inglese
flower bed	l'aiuola
vegetable garden	l'orto
greenhouse	la serra
swimming pool	la piscina
barbecue	il barbecue
tennis court	il campo da tennis
the situation	la situazione / l'ubicazione
aspect	l'aspetto / l'esposizione
view	la vista / la veduta
stone	la pietra
brick	il mattone
timber	il legname
concrete	il calcestruzzo

Useful verbs

to buy	comprare
to sell	vendere
to view (a house)	vedere
to make an appointment	prendere un appuntamento
to lock up	chiudere a chiave

Useful phrases

it overlooks the bay	dà sulla baia
a central position	una posizione centrale
close to all services	vicino ai servizi
in the town centre	nel centro città
in the suburbs	in periferia
in the country	in campagna

5.2 Rooms

Core vocabulary

rooms	le camere
entrance / hall	l'ingresso
kitchen	la cucina
dining room	la sala da pranzo
sitting room	il salotto / soggiorno
bedroom	la camera da letto
play room	la stanza dei giochi
bath room	la stanza da bagno
cloak room (downstairs toilet)	la toilette
study / office	lo studio
landing	il pianerottolo
stairs	la scala
junk room	il ripostiglio
window	la finestra
radiator	il radiatore
floor	il pavimento
ceiling	il tetto
door	la porta
wall	il muro / la parete
window sill	il davanzale
central heating	il riscaldamento
water heater	lo scaldacqua / lo scaldabagno
lock	la serratura
key	la chiave
plug	la spina
socket	la presa di corrente
switch	l'interruttore
handle	la maniglia
fuse box	la cassetta dei fusibili
fuse	il fusibile
fuse wire	il filo fusibile
torch	la torcia elettrica
curtains	le tende
blinds	le veneziane
shutters	le imposte

carpet / rug	il tappeto
fitted carpet	la moquette
floor/wall tiles	le mattonelle / piastrelle
flooring	il materiale per pavimentazioni
wallpaper	la tappezzeria
paint	la vernice
paintbrush	il pennello
ladder	la scala a pioli
step ladder	la scala a libretto

Useful phrases

upstairs	al piano di sopra
downstairs	al pianterreno
on the first floor	al primo piano
in the basement	nel seminterrato
in the attic	nella mansarda
Where is the ...?	Dov'è il/la ...?
How does it work?	Come funziona?

Useful verbs

to turn / switch on	accendere
to turn / switch off	spegnere

5.3 Furniture

Core vocabulary

furniture	i mobili
in the sitting room	nel salotto / soggiorno
armchair / easy chair	la poltrona
settee / sofa	il divano
coffee table	il tavolino
bookcase	la libreria / lo scaffale
lamp	la lampada
pictures	i quadri

in the bedroom	nella camera da letto
bed	il letto
bedside table	il comodino
chair	la sedia
wardrobe	l'armadio
chest of drawers	il comò / cassettone

mirror	lo specchio
built in cupboard	l'armadio a muro
shelves	le mensole
in the bathroom	nella stanza da bagno
bath	il bagno
razor	il rasoio
shower	la doccia
wash basin	il lavabo / lavandino
toilet	il gabinetto / bagno
toilet (bowl)	il vaso del gabinetto
toothbrush	lo spazzolino da denti
toothpaste	il dentifricio

5.4 Household goods

Core vocabulary

television	la televisione
television set	il televisore
video recorder	il videoregistratore
DVD player	il lettore di DVD
remote control	il telecomando
bedding	le coperte e lenzuola
pillow / pillow case	il cuscino / la federa
quilt	il piumino
quilt cover	la federa del piumino
sheet	il lenzuolo
fitted sheet	il lenzuolo con gli angoli
taps	i rubinetti
plug	il tappo
shampoo	lo shampoo
conditioner	il balsamo
hair dryer	l'asciugacapelli
soap	il sapone
towel	l'asciugamano
deodorant	il deodorante
vacuum cleaner	l'aspirapolvere (m)
duster	lo straccio per la polvere
brush	la spazzola
dustpan	la paletta
cleaning materials	i materiali per la pulizia
scrubbing brush	lo spazzolone

| *floor mop* | il mocio |
| *detergent* | il detersivo / detergente |

Useful phrases

Where is the ...?	Dov'è il/la ...?
It's on the table	È sul tavolo
under the bed	sotto il letto
in the armchair	nella poltrona
in the cupboard / drawer	nell'armadio / nel cassetto
Can I have a clean ...?	Mi può dare un/a ... pulito/a?
How does the (television) work?	Come funziona questo televisore?

Useful verbs

to do housework	fare i lavori di casa
to wash	lavare
to clean	pulire
to vacuum	pulire con l'aspirapolvere
to make the beds	fare il letto

5.5 In the kitchen

Core vocabulary

table	il tavolo
chair	la sedia
stool	lo sgabello
drawer	il cassetto
cupboard	l'armadio
shelf	la mensola
sink	il lavello / l'acquaio
fridge	il frigo(rifero)
dishwasher	la lavastoviglie
washing machine	la lavatrice
drier	l'asciugabiancheria
mixer / liquidizer	il frullatore
plate	il piatto
dinner plate	il piatto piano
bowl	la scodella / coppetta
salad bowl	l'insalatiera
dish	il piatto
cup	la tazza
saucer	il piattino

mug	il tazzone
jug	la caraffa
teapot	la teiera
sugar bowl	la zuccheriera
knife	il coltello
fork	la forchetta
spoon	il cucchiaio
teaspoon	il cucchiaino
soup spoon	il cucchiaio da minestra
dessert spoon	il cucchiaio da dessert
carving knife	il trinciante
bread knife	il coltello per il pane
vegetable knife	il coltello per pelare le verdure
sharp	affilato
glass	il bicchiere
wineglass	il bicchiere da vino
champagne glass	il bicchiere da champagne
water glass	il bicchiere per l'acqua
tumbler	il bicchiere
salt	il sale
pepper	il pepe
mustard	la senape / la mostarda

Useful phrases

I like / dislike cooking	mi piace / non mi piace cucinare
I'll do the washing up	io laverò i piatti

Useful verbs

ℹ️
- In recipes, instructions are usually given in the infinitive form of the verb as in the following list.
- If a friend gives you instructions they will use the normal **tu** form ending in **-i** for **-ere** (**batti**) and **-ire** (**arrostisci**) verbs and a special form ending in **-a** for **-are** verbs (**mescola**).
- See also p. 113.

mix	mescolare
beat	battere
roast	arrostire
toast	tostare
bake	cuocere (al forno)
steam	cuocere a vapore
grill	cuocere ai ferri / alla griglia
barbecue	cuocere alla brace
peel	pelare / sbucciare

cut	tagliare
slice	tagliare a fette
chop	tagliare a pezzetti
fry	friggere
slightly fry	soffriggere

rubbish *la spazzatura*

left-overs	gli avanzi
packaging	la confezione / l'imballaggio
plastic bags	i sacchetti di plastica
kitchen bin / waste bin	la pattumiera
bin liner / black bag	il sacco di plastica per la spazzatura
dustbin	il bidone della spazzatura
recycling	il riciclaggio
bottle bank	il contenitore per la raccolta del vetro
compost	il concime

5.6 Outside

Core vocabulary

garage	il garage
shed	il capanno
footpath	il sentiero
gate	il cancello / il portone
security code	il codice di sicurezza
in the garden	in giardino
flower bed	l'aiuola
lawn	il prato all'inglese
flower	il fiore
plant	la pianta
bush / shrub	il cespuglio / l'arbusto
tree	l'albero
grass	l'erba
weeds	le erbacce
herbs	le erbe aromatiche
bulbs	i bulbi

trees *gli alberi*

beech	il faggio
chestnut	il castagno
elm	l'olmo

hazel	il nocciolo
holly	l'agrifoglio
oak	la quercia
sycamore	il sicomoro
willow	il salice
poplar	il pioppo
cypress	il cipresso

flowers *i fiori*

carnation	il garofano
daffodil	il trombone / la giunchiglia
rose	la rosa
sweet pea	il pisello odoroso
tulip	il tulipano
mimosa	la mimosa
orange-blossom	il fiore d'arancio

garden tools *gli attrezzi da giardinaggio*

fork	la forca
hoe	la zappa
rake	il rastrello
spade	la vanga
trowel	la paletta da giardiniere
lawnmower	il tagliaerba
wheelbarrow	la carriola
garden tractor	il trattore da giardino
garden cultivator / rotavator	il coltivatore
hose	il tubo per annaffiare
sprinkler	l'irrigatore
watering can	l'annaffiatoio
weed-killer	il diserbante / l'erbicida
fertilizer	il fertilizzante

insects and pests *gli insetti e gli animali nocivi*

ant	la formica
bee	l'ape (f)
greenfly	l'afide (m)
housefly	la mosca
mosquito	la zanzara
spider	il ragno
wasp	la vespa

i You must have seen the word **Vespa** used for a make of scooter. It isn't hard to guess why it is so called!

garden furniture *i mobili da giardino*

barbecue	il barbecue
table	il tavolo
deck chair	la sedia a sdraio
lounger	il lettino da spiaggia
bench	la panchina
swing	l'altalena
slide	lo scivolo

Useful phrases

it needs to be weeded	c'è bisogno di diserbarlo
it needs to be watered	c'è bisogno di annaffiarlo
the grass needs to be cut	bisogna tagliare l'erba
they are ripe / not ripe	sono / non sono maturi
I like / dislike gardening	mi piace / non mi piace il giardinaggio
He/she has green fingers	Lui/lei ha il pollice verde
I am allergic to ...	sono allergico a ...
I have been stung!	Sono stato punto!

Useful verbs

to dig	scavare
to plant	piantare
to grow	coltivare
to weed	diserbare
to water	annaffiare
to pick	(rac)cogliere
to cut the grass	tagliare l'erba

5.7 Tools and DIY

Core vocabulary

drill	il trapano
(drill) bits	le punte
hammer	il martello
pincers	le tenaglie
pliers	le pinze
saw	la sega
chain saw	la motosega
screwdriver	il cacciavite
spanner	la chiave inglese

staple gun	la pistola sparachiodi
tape measure	il metro a nastro
nail	il chiodo
bolt	il bullone
nut	il dado
staple	il punto metallico
brush	la spazzola
paint brush	il pennello
scissors	le forbici
sandpaper	la carta vetrata
ladder	la scala a pioli
scaffold	l'impalcatura
tiles	le tegole (*roof*); le piastrelle (*floor*)
slates	le tegole d'ardesia
window pane	il vetro
window frame	il telaio della finestra
sliding window	la finestra a ghigliottina
shutters	le imposte
plumbing and electricity	le tubature e l'elettricità
pipe	la tubatura
tap	il rubinetto
wire	il filo (elettrico)
fuse	il fusibile
plug	la spina
socket	la presa di corrente

Useful phrases

Can you fix it?	Puoi / può ripararlo?
Yes I can!	Sì, certo!
to fix something to a wall	attaccare / fissare qualche cosa al muro
to fix /mend	sistemare / riparare
DIY	il bricolage / fai da te
DIY shop	il negozio di bricolage

Useful verbs

to screw	avvitare
to unscrew	svitare
to hammer	martellare
to nail	inchiodare

to *drill*	forare / trapanare
to *fasten*	legare / fissare
to *cut*	tagliare
to *rub down (sandpaper)*	levigare (con carta vetrata)
to *paint*	verniciare
to *plane*	piallare
to *glue*	incollare
to *solder*	saldare
to *weld*	saldare

06

food and drink

6.1 Parties and celebrations

Core vocabulary

an invitation	un invito
a reply	una risposta
an acceptance	un'accettazione
a refusal	un rifiuto
an excuse	un pretesto
a cake	un dolce / una torta
champagne	lo champagne
a toast	un brindisi
a present	un regalo
Cheers!	Salute! / Cin cin!

Useful phrases

let's have a party	diamo una festa
let's dance	balliamo
I would like to propose a toast	vorrei proporre un brindisi
I would like to thank our hosts	vorrei ringraziare i nostri ospiti
I've got a hangover	soffro i postumi della sbornia

Useful verbs

to party	dare una festa
to eat	mangiare
to drink	bere
to toast (the bride)	proporre un brindisi (alla sposa)
to enjoy oneself	divertirsi
to overindulge / have too much	mangiare / bere troppo
to get drunk	ubriacarsi
to feel sick	avere nausea, sentirsi la nausea

i It is customary to take a gift to one's host or hostess when visiting a home in Italy; a popular choice is a selection of **pasticceria** *little cakes*.

6.2 Mealtimes

i Mealtimes and eating habits in Italy are as follows:

- **la prima colazione** *breakfast* is light: usually coffee, fruit-juice, a pastry, biscuits or toast; children often have chocolate spread such as **Nutella** on bread or toast, but cereals and milk are becoming increasingly popular.
- Many people go out from work to a bar mid-morning for coffee and a bun.
- **il pranzo** *lunch* is the main meal of the day; any time from about 1 to 3 pm; usually 2/3 courses, beginning with e.g. a starter or fish, then main course, but vegetables/salad separate; often fruit for dessert; perhaps accompanied by wine, especially at weekends; often followed by *a snooze* **la siesta** if possible!
- **la cena** *dinner*; can be at any time from about 7 pm to midnight! usually a lighter meal than lunch, unless a special occasion.

Core vocabulary

meals	i pasti
mealtimes	le ore dei pasti
breakfast	la prima colazione
lunch	la colazione
picnic basket	il cestino per il picnic
dinner	il pranzo
supper	la cena
the menu	la carta / il menù
starter	antipasto
first course	il primo piatto
soup	la zuppa / la minestra
fish	il pesce
main course	il piatto principale / forte
side dish	il contorno
dessert	il dolce
cheese	il formaggio
coffee	il caffè

drinks *le bevande*

soft drink	la bibita analcolica
orange juice	il succo d'arancia
water	l'acqua (f)
mineral water	l'acqua minerale
fizzy	gassosa / frizzante
still	naturale / non gassosa

aperitif	l'aperitivo (m)
cocktail	il cocktail
sherry	lo sherry
gin and tonic	il gin tonic
red wine	il vino rosso
white wine	il vino bianco
champagne	lo champagne
brandy	il brandy
liqueur	il liquore

starters *antipasti*

| starters / hors d'oeuvres | antipasti |
| mixed starters | antipasti misti |

first courses *primi piatti*

fish soup	la zuppa di pesce
minestrone	il minestrone
chicken soup	la zuppa di pollo
mushroom soup	la zuppa di funghi
pasta and beans in thick soup	la pasta fagioli
mushroom risotto	il risotto ai funghi
spaghetti with tomato sauce	gli spaghetti al pomodoro
tortellini – small filled envelopes of pasta	i tortellini
cannelloni – pasta tubes	i cannelloni
lasagna – layered pasta	le lasagne
gnocchi – small potato pasta dumplings	i gnocchi

fish and meat *il pesce e la carne*

veal	il vitello
beef	il manzo
pork	la carne di maiale
lamb	l'agnello (m)

See also p. 111–12

vegetables *la verdura*

beans	i fagioli
peas	i pisellini
artichoke	il carciofo
fennel	il finocchio
cabbage	il cavolo
potatoes	le patate
chips	le patate fritte

See also p. 110.

desserts *i dolci*

cream	la panna
zabaglione	lo zabaglione (*creamy dessert made of egg yolks, sugar and marsala*)
tiramisu	il tiramisù (*sponge soaked in coffee, topped with cream cheese and chocolate*)
ice cream	il gelato
flavours of ice-cream	gusti di gelato
coconut	il cocco
pistachio	il pistacchio
strawberry	la fragola
raspberry	il lampone
vanilla	la vaniglia
lemon	il limone
chocolate	il cioccolato

coffee and tea *il caffè e il tè*

coffee	il caffè
coffee without milk	il caffè
strong black coffee	il caffè ristretto
weak black coffee	il caffè lungo
espresso	l'espresso
small espresso	il caffè corto
coffee with spirits	il caffè corretto
coffee with milk	il caffelatte
coffee with a dash of milk	il caffè macchiato
cappuccino	il cappuccino cappuccio (*slang*)
decaffeinated coffee	il caffè decaffeinato
with sugar	con lo zucchero
with sweetener	con dolcificante
senza zucchero	without sugar
tea	il tè
Indian tea	il tè indiano
China tea	il tè cinese
herbal tea	l'infusione di erbe
with milk	con latte
with lemon	con limone
with sugar	con zucchero

Useful phrases

I *have a special diet*	seguo una dieta speciale
I *am allergic to*	sono allergico a
I *don't eat* ...	non mangio ...
I *can't eat* ...	non posso mangiare ...
I *am a vegan*	sono vegetaliano
I *am a vegetarian*	sono vegetariano
I *am diabetic*	sono diabetico

Useful verbs

to *like / dislike*	piacere / non piacere/a
I *like ... (it pleases me)*	mi piace ...
I *like ... (they please me)*	mi piacciono ...
to *eat*	mangiare
to *drink*	bere
to *prefer*	preferire
to *love*	amare

6.3 Breakfast

Core vocabulary

breakfast	la prima colazione
cereals	i cereali
wheat	il grano / frumento
oats	l'avena
barley	l'orzo
rye	la segale
bran	la crusca
cornflakes	i cornflakes / fiocchetti
muesli	il müsli
milk	il latte
semi-skimmed milk	il latte parzialmente scremato
fat free milk	il latte scremato
soya milk	il latte di soia
goat's milk	il latte di capra
cream	la panna
yoghurt	lo yogurt
bacon	la pancetta
eggs	le uova*
scrambled eggs	uova strapazzate
poached eggs	uova in camicia

boiled eggs	uova alla coque
hard boiled eggs	uova sode
fried eggs	uova fritte

*L'uovo is masculine in the singular, feminine in the plural le uova.

sausages	le salsicce
tomato	il pomodoro
mushrooms	i funghi
fried	fritti
grilled	alla griglia
tinned	in scatola
baked beans	i fagioli all'uccelletto
pancake	la frittella
maple syrup	lo sciroppo d'acero
ham	il prosciutto
salami	i salumi
cheese	il formaggio
bread	il pane
white	bianco
brown	integrale / nero
granary	con chicchi di grano interi
wholemeal	integrale
sliced	a cassetta / a fette
organic	biologico
rolls	i panini
croissant	il croissant / cornetto
Danish pastries	la pasticceria
butter	il burro
margarine	la margarina
low fat spread	la margarina magra
jam	la marmellata / confettura
marmalade	la marmellata d'arance
honey	il miele
peanut butter	il burro d'arachidi
tea	il tè
coffee	il caffè
milk	il latte
cold milk	il latte fresco
hot milk	il latte freddo
hot chocolate	la cioccolata calda
fruit juice	il succo di frutta
orange juice	il succo d'arancia
freshly squeezed orange juice	la spremuta d'arancia

Useful phrases

I *don't eat breakfast*	non faccio la prima colazione
I *only eat* ...	mangio solo ...
I *don't drink milk*	non bevo il latte
I *have my breakfast at* ...	faccio la prima colazione alle ...

6.4 Snacks

Core vocabulary

yoghurt	lo yogurt
biscuit	il biscotto
chocolate biscuit	il biscotto al cioccolato
piece of cake	una fetta di torta
bun	il panino dolce
sweets (desserts)	i dolci
sweets (e.g. toffees)	le caramelle
sandwich	il tramezzino / sandwich / panino
in brown bread	di pane integrale
in white bread	di pane bianco
in a roll	*in* un panino
with/without mayonnaise	con/senza maionese
with/without salad dressing	con/senza condimento
salad	un'insalata
green salad	un'insalata verde
tomato salad	un'insalata di pomodori
mixed salad	un'insalata mista
Russian salad	un'insalata russa
potato salad	un'insalata di patate
pancake	la frittella / crêpe
pasta	la pasta
spaghetti	gli spaghetti
lasagne	le lasagne
pizza	la pizza
fish and chips	il pesce con patate fritte
a (ham)burger	l'hamburger
a cheeseburger	il cheesburger

Useful phrases

Can I offer you a cup of coffee?	Vuoi / Vuole un caffè?
How do you take it?	Come lo prendi / prende?
With milk or without milk?	Con latte o senza?
Do you take sugar?	Lo prendi / prende con zucchero?
Have you got a sweetener?	Hai / Ha un dolcificante?
Would you like a biscuit?	Ti/Le piacerebbe un biscotto?
Yes, please	Sì, per favore
No, thank you	No, grazie
I am on a diet	Sono a dieta
I don't take ...	Non prendo ...
It's too hot / cold / spicy	È troppo caldo / freddo / piccante
It isn't cooked properly	Non è cucinato bene
It is delicious!	È delizioso!

6.5 Fruit and vegetables

fruit *la frutta*

apple	la mela
cooking apple	la mela da cuocere
dessert apple	la mela da mangiare
apricot	l'albicocca
banana	la banana
fig	il fico
grapes	l'uva
cherries	le ciliege
melon	il melone
watermelon	il cocomero / l'anguria
peach	la pesca
pear	la pera
plum	la prugna
raspberry	il lampone
rhubarb	il rabarbaro
strawberry	la fragola

citrus fruits *gli agrumi*

grapefruit	il pompelmo
lemon	il limone
lime	il cedro
orange	l'arancia

berries *le bacche*

blackcurrant	il ribes nero
blueberry / bilberry / cranberry	il mirtillo
gooseberry	l'uva spina
redcurrant	il ribes rosso

exotic fruits *i frutti esotici*

avocado	l'avocado
coconut	la noce di cocco
dates	il dattero
kiwi fruit	il kiwi
mango	il mango
passion fruit	il frutto della passione
pineapple	l'ananas

nuts *frutta secca*

almond	la mandorla
brazil	la noce del Brasile
cashew	l'anacardio
hazelnut	la nocciola
peanut	l'arachide (f)
pistachio	il pistacchio
walnut	la noce
raisin	l'uvetta
sultana	l'uva sultanina
candied peel	la frutta candita

vegetables *la verdura*

cucumber	il cetriolo
lettuce	la lattuga
radish	il ravanello
spring onion	la cipollina
tomatoes	i pomodori
beans	i fagioli
broccoli	i broccoli
cabbage	il cavolo
carrot	la carota
cauliflower	il cavolfiore
courgette	lo zucchino
pepper	il peperone
aubergine	la melanzana
garlic	l'aglio
leek	il porro
lettuce	la lattuga

mushroom	il fungo (pl funghi)
onion	la cipolla
potato	la patata
sweetcorn	il mais
turnip / swede	la rapa (svedese)
kidney beans	i fagioli comuni
French / green / runner beans	i fagiolini
broad beans	le fave
lentils	le lenticchie
pumpkin	la zucca
shallots	gli scalogni
spinach	gli spinaci
watercress	il crescione

6.6 Fish and meat

salt water fish *il pesce di mare*

anchovy	l'acciuga / alice (f)
cod	il merluzzo
haddock	l'eglefino
herring	l'aringa
mackerel	lo sgombro
plaice	la passera
sardine	la sardina
skate	la razza
sole	la sogliola
tuna	il tonno
hake	il nasello
jelly fish	la medusa
octopus	il polpo
red mullet	la triglia
sea bass	il branzino
squid	il calamaro
whiting	il merlango

shellfish *i frutti di mare*

crab	il granchio
langoustine / lobster	l'aragosta
mussels	le cozze
oyster	l'ostrica
prawn	il gambero / gamberetto

fresh water fish *il pesce d'acqua dolce*

trout	la trota
salmon	il salmone
perch	il pesce persico
pike	il luccio
eel	l'anguilla

meat *la carne*

beef	il manzo
lamb	l'agnello
pork	il maiale
veal	il vitello
ham	il prosciutto
liver	il fegato
kidneys	i rognoni

poultry *il pollame*

chicken	il pollo
turkey	il tacchino
duck	l'anatra
goose	l'oca

game *la selvaggina*

grouse	l'urogallo / il gallo cedrone
hare	la lepre
partridge	la pernice
pheasant	il fagiano
pigeon	il piccione
rabbit	il coniglio
venison	la carne di cervo
wild boar	il cinghiale

i The two most famous Italian cheeses are **parmigiano** (*parmesan*) made from sheep's milk and often sprinkled in grated form on pasta; and **gorgonzola**, a creamy blue cheese which tastes far better than you'd think. In recent times, **mozzarella** (in authentic form made from buffalo milk) has been made popular by the pizza; among other great cheeses to look out for are **ricotta** a very creamy, soft cheese, and **provolone**, a mature hard cheese, often sold in its spicy form as **provolone piccante**.

6.7 Using a recipe

making a cake *fare una torta*

ingredients	gli ingredienti
flour	la farina
plain flour	la farina
self-raising flour	la farina con lievito
raising agent (baking powder)	il lievito
cornflour / potato flour	la fecola di patate
sugar	lo zucchero
butter	il burro
salt	il sale
vanilla	la vaniglia
almond essence	l'essenza di mandorla
melted chocolate	il cioccolato fuso
grated lemon rind	la scorza di limone grattugiata
the juice of an orange	il succo di un'arancia
chopped walnuts, hazlenuts, almonds	le noci, nocciole, mandorle tritate
grated chocolate	il cioccolato grattugiato
scales	la bilancia
mixing bowl	la terrina
wooden spoon	il cucchiaio di legno
mixer	il frullatore / mixer
grater	la grattugia
sieve	il setaccio
baking tin	la tortiera / lo stampo
oven	il forno
oven gloves	i guanti da forno

making soup *fare la zuppa / la minestra*

prepare the vegetables	preparare la verdura
peel the carrots	sbucciare / pelare le carote
chop the leeks	tagliare i porri
melt the butter	fondere il burro
add the flour	aggiungere la farina
stir the mixture	mescolare / agitare la mistura
pour in the stock	versare il brodo
saucepan	la casseruola / pentola
casserole	la casseruola
frying pan	la padella
lid	il coperchio

handle	il manico
silver foil	la carta di alluminio / stagnola
cling film	la pellicola trasparente
greaseproof paper	la carta oleata
plastic bags	i sacchetti di plastica
plastic containers	i recipienti di plastica

Useful verbs

heat	riscaldare
cook	cucinare
roast	arrostire
bake	cuocere (al forno)
fry	friggere
boil	(far) bollire
poach	affogare / cuocere in bianco / lessare

7
in town

7.1 The town plan and the sights

Core vocabulary

bank	la banca
bus station	la stazione degli autobus / l'autostazione
car park	il parcheggio
cinema	il cinema
football ground	il campo di calcio
hospital	l'ospedale
hotel	l'albergo
library	la biblioteca
market	il mercato
post office	l'ufficio postale / la posta
station	la stazione
swimming pool	la piscina
tourist office	l'ufficio turistico
town hall	il municipio
the sights	i monumenti
bridge	il ponte
castle	il castello
cathedral	il duomo / la cattedrale
church	la chiesa
fountain	la fontana
monument	il monumento
museum	il museo
old town	la città vecchia / il centro storico
opera house	il teatro dell'opera / il teatro lirico
park	il parco
river	il fiume
square	la piazza
statue	la statua
theatre	il teatro
region	la regione
district	il quartiere
built-up area	il centro abitato / l'abitato
town	il Paese / la città
suburbs	i sobborghi / la periferia
town centre	il centro (città)

industrial zone	la zona industriale
council offices	gli uffici municipali
law courts	i tribunali / le corti di giustizia
museum	il museo
police station	il commissariato
opening times	l'orario di apertura
open	aperto/a
closed	chiuso/a
holidays	le vacanze
bank holiday	il giorno di festa civile
annual holiday	le ferie annuali

Useful verbs

to meet	incontrarsi / vedersi
to look for	cercare
to be situated	essere situato/a

Useful phrases

Let's meet at the café Roma	Ci vediamo / incontriamo al caffè Roma
Where is it?	Dov'è?
It is in the centre	È in centro
on the main street	sulla strada principale
near the post office	vicino alla posta
opposite the bank	di fronte alla banca
on the market place	sulla piazza del mercato
beside the river	in riva al fiume

i If you ring up to find out when the bank is open, this is the sort of message you might hear:

La banca è aperta dalle 9 alle 2 e dalle 4 alle 6 da martedì a venerdì, e dalle 9 alle 2 il sabato. La banca è chiusa il lunedì.

If you ring up to find out what is on at the cinema, this is what you might hear:

Oggi diamo il nuovo film di Roberto Benigni, 'Pinocchio'. Ci sono spettacoli alle 6, alle 8.30 e alle 11. Abbiamo biglietti da 10 euro e da 15 euro.

7.2 Getting around town

Core vocabulary

road (*between towns*)	la strada
road / street (*in towns*)	la via
avenue	il corso / viale
pavement	il marciapiede
gutter	il canale di scolo
pedestrian crossing	il passaggio pedonale
pedestrian zone	la zona pedonale
traffic lights	il semaforo
crossing lights	le luci del passaggio pedonale
"green man"	il segnale di via libera
subway (*foot passage*)	il sottopassaggio

How do I get into town? *Come posso andare in città?*

by car	in macchina / con la macchina
by bus	in autobus / con l'autobus
by tram	in tram / con il tram
by subway (*metro*)	in / con la metropolitana / in / con il metrò

Where is ...? *Dov'è ...?*

the bus stop	la fermata d'autobus
the subway/tube station	la stazione del metrò

parking the car *parcheggiare la macchina*

car park	il parcheggio
multi-storey car park	il parcheggio a più piani
underground car park	il parcheggio sotterraneo
full	completo / pieno
spaces	posti
entrance	l'entrata
ticket machine	il distributore (automatico) di biglietti
change (*coinage*)	la moneta / gli spiccioli
change (*money returned*)	il resto
credit card	la carta di credito
ticket	il biglietto
exit	l'uscita
barrier	la barriera
traffic warden	il vigile urbano
one-way system	il senso unico

Useful phrases

Use the crossing	Usare il passaggio pedonale
Don't cross	Non attraversare
There's a car coming	Arriva una macchina
Wait for the green man	Aspettare la luce verde
jay walking	attraversare la strada fuori dai passaggi consentiti
Excuse me ...	Mi scusi ...
Can you tell me ...?	Mi sa dire...? / Può dirmi...?
How do I get to the station?	Per andare alla stazione?
Where is the nearest car park?	Dov'è il parcheggio più vicino?
When is the next bus?	A che ora passa il prossimo autobus?
It is forbidden ...	È proibito...
to cross the road here	attraversare la strada qui
to drop litter	lasciar cadere rifiuti / cartacce
to park	parcheggiare

Useful verbs

to walk	andare a piedi
to cross	attraversare
to turn left / right	girare a sinistra / destra
to go straight on	andare sempre dritto / diritto
to run	correre
to drive	andare in macchina
to catch the bus	prendere l'autobus
to miss the bus	perdere l'autobus

7.3 Shops and shopping

Core vocabulary

shops	i negozi
bakery / at the baker's	la panetteria / dal panettiere / dal fornaio
butcher	il macellaio
cake shop	la pasticceria
chemist	la farmacia
clothes shop	il negozio di abbigliamento
department store	il grande magazzino
flower shop	il fioraio / il negozio di fiori

hairdresser	il parrucchiere
hypermarket	l'ipermercato
market	il mercato
shoe shop	il negozio di scarpe / calzature
shopping centre / mall	il centro commerciale
sports shop	il negozio dello sport
supermarket	il supermercato
sweet-shop / confectioners	il negozio di dolciumi / la pasticceria
health food store	il negozio di cibo macrobiotico
newsagent's	l'agenzia di stampa
optician	l'optometrista / ottico
dry cleaner's	la tintoria
travel agent	l'agenzia di viaggi
photographic shop	il negozio di materiale fotografico
card shop	il negozio di biglietti d'auguri
store guide	la guida del grande magazzino
escalator	la scala mobile
lift	l'ascensore
ground floor	il pianterreno
first floor	il primo piano
bedding	le coperte e lenzuole
fashion	la moda
sportswear	l'abbigliamento sportivo
casual wear	il casual
leather goods	(gli articoli di) pelletteria
television and electrical goods	televisione ed elettrodomestici
sales person	il commesso / la commessa
cash desk	la cassa
changing room	il camerino
customer, client	il/la cliente
price	il prezzo
deposit	l'acconto
discount	lo sconto
reductions / sales	riduzioni / saldi
reduced prices	prezzi ridotti / grandi ribassi
clearance / closing down sale	svendita / (vendita di) liquidazione
bargain (offers)	affari / occasioni

Useful phrases

How much does it cost?	Quanto costa?
How are you paying?	Come vuole pagare?
Are you paying cash?	Paga in contanti?
Do you have the right change?	Ha gli spiccioli esatti?
Will you wrap it as a gift?	Lo può incartare in confezione regalo?
out of stock	esaurito

Useful verbs

to buy	comprare
to sell	vendere
to look for	cercare
to pay	pagare
to prefer	preferire
to go shopping	andare a fare la spesa / lo shopping
to order	ordinare
to deliver	consegnare
to window shop	andare a vedere le vetrine

7.4 At the supermarket

Core vocabulary

food department	il reparto di alimentari
fruit and vegetables	frutta e verdura
dairy products	latticini
frozen foods	prodotti surgelati
cleaning materials	prodotti per le pulizie
electrical goods	articoli elettrici
household appliances	elettrodomestici
CDs	i CD
videos	i video
wines and spirits	vini e liquori
drinks	bibite
bottle of water	la bottiglia d'acqua
jar of jam	il vasetto di marmellata
box of paper hankies	la scatola di fazzolettini di carta
tin of tomatoes	la scatola di pomodori
packet of biscuits	il pacchetto di biscotti
tube of toothpaste	il tubetto di dentifricio

assistant	il commesso / la commessa
basket	il cestino
trolley	il carrello
cashier	il cassiere / la cassiera
check out	la cassa

Useful verbs

to buy	comprare
to sell	vendere
to weigh	pesare
to look for	cercare
to find	trovare
to deliver	consegnare

Useful phrases

Where is / Where are …?	Dov'è / Dove sono …?
on the aisle	nel passaggio / nella corsia
on the shelf	sul ripiano

Where is the gardening section?	Dov'è il reparto di giardinaggio
on the row with the …	nel passaggio con il/la …
at the far end	in fondo
on the left/right hand side	a sinistra / destra

Is there a restaurant?	C'è un ristorante?
What time do you shut?	A che ora chiudete?
Are you open on a Sunday?	È aperto la domenica?

i Italian supermarkets and hypermarkets are no different from ours, except that there are more giant shops with an extremely wide range of products, and such out-of town hypermarkets have lots of 'satellite shops' under the same roof.

7.5 At the post office and the bank

Core vocabulary

the post office *l'ufficio postale*

letter box	la cassetta delle lettere
post	la posta
letter	la lettera
packet	il pacchetto
parcel	il pacchetto / il pacco

postcard	la cartolina (postale)
writing paper	la carta da lettere
envelope	la busta
form	il modulo
stamp	il francobollo
postman	il postino
phone card	la scheda telefonica
printed matter	le stampe
recorded delivery	la lettera raccomandata
overnight delivery	la consegna da un giorno all'altro
air mail	la posta aerea
e-mail	la posta elettronica

i Stamps can be bought not only at a post-office, but also in stationery shops, in shops which sell postcards, at newsagents and tobacconists.

the bank *la banca*

money	i soldi
cash	i contanti
coins	le monete
notes	le banconote
cheque book	il libretto degli assegni
credit card	la carta di credito

i In Italian banks, it is normal to have to cash a cheque or traveller's cheque at one desk and to take the docket to another actually to draw the cash; nowadays, however, this should be unnecessary, as almost every bank has a cash dispenser **sportello automatico** or **bancomat**. Just make sure you are familiar with the **euro**!

cash machine	lo sportello automatico / il bancomat
a cash transfer	il trasferimento bancario / il bonifico
the date	la data
the amount	la quantità
signature	la firma
the bank code	il numero d'agenzia della banca
the credit card number	il numero della carta di credito
the expiry date	la data di scadenza
balance	il saldo
loan	il prestito
mortgage	il mutuo ipotecario

Useful phrases

insert your card	inserire la carta
type in your number	digitare il numero
wait	attendere
remove your card	togliere la carta
take your money	prendere i soldi
fill in the form	riempire il modulo
go to the counter/ cash desk	andare alla cassa
Where do I have to sign?	Dove devo firmare?
How much does it cost to send this to ...?	Quanto costa spedire questo a ...?

Useful verbs

to cash	incassare
to deposit	depositare
to transfer	trasferire
to sign	firmare
to fill in	riempire

08

in the country

8.1 The countryside

Core vocabulary

in the countryside	in campagna
field	il campo
meadow	il prato
footpath	il sentiero
hill	la collina
mountain	la montagna
stream	il ruscello
river	il fiume
lake	il lago
valley	la valle
grass	l'erba
plant	la pianta
wild flower	i fiori selvatici
moss	il muschio
fungi	i funghi / le muffe
fern	la felce
bush	il cespuglio
tree	l'albero
wood	il bosco
forest	la selva / foresta
hedge	la siepe
fence	lo steccato / il recinto
ditch	il fosso
gate	il cancello
spring	la sorgente
pond	lo stagno
bridge	il ponte
waterfall	la cascata
weir	lo sbarramento
water mill	il mulino ad acqua
reservoir	il bacino idrico
dam	la diga
hydro electric power station	la centrale idroelettrica
flood	l'inondazione, lo straripamento
copse	il boschetto
beech	il faggio
chestnut tree	il castagno
elm	l'olmo

oak	la quercia
sycamore	il sicomoro
willow	il salice

Useful phrases

| Where shall we go? | Dove andiamo? |
| What shall we do? | Cosa facciamo? |

Useful verbs

to go for a walk	andare a fare quattro passi
to go for a long walk	andare a fare una lunga passeggiata
to go swimming	andare a nuotare
to swim	nuotare
to go hiking	fare un'escursione a piedi
to ride a bike	andare in bicicletta
to go fishing	pescare / andare a pesca
to flood	inondare / straripare

8.2 In the mountains

Core vocabulary

hill	la collina
mountain	la montagna
mountain range	la catena di montagne
mountain pass	il passo / la gola
mountain path	il sentiero di montagna
mountain railway	la funicolare
mountain hut / refuge	il rifugio di montaga
cable car	la funivia
summit	la cima
peak	la cima / la vetta
rock face	la parete di roccia
slope	il pendio / versante
gorge	la gola
cave	la caverna

the weather il tempo

| cloudy | nuvoloso |
| rainy | piovoso |

sunny	soleggiato / assolato
it's sunny	c'è il sole
dry	secco
windy	ventoso
it's windy	c'è vento
easy	facile
of moderate difficulty	abbastanza difficile
difficult	difficile
of extreme difficulty	di estrema difficoltà

equipment *l'attrezzatura*

rope	la corda / la fune
harness	l'imbracatura
karabiner	il moschettone
rucksack	lo zaino / il sacco da montagna
torch	la torcia elettrica / lampadina tascabile
stove	la cucina / stufa
dried food	alimenti liofilizzati / disidratati
waterproofs	gli impermeabili
pen knife	il temperino
water bottle	la borraccia
sleeping bag	il sacco a pelo
tent	la tenda

Useful verbs

to climb	salire
to abseil	discendere a corda doppia
to bivouac	bivaccare
to hike	fare un'escursione a piedi
to rock climb	fare roccia
to boulder	arrampicarsi su massi / fare sassismo
to ice climb	arrampicarsi su ghiaccio

Useful phrases

What is the forecast?	Come sono le previsioni del tempo?
How difficult is it?	Quant'è difficile?
How long does it take?	Quanto tempo ci vuole?

8.3 At the seaside

Core vocabulary

sea-side (resort)	la stazione balneare
at the seaside	al mare
sea	il mare
ocean	l'oceano
wave	l'onda
harbour / port	il porto
beach	la spiaggia
sand	la sabbia
sand dune	la duna (di sabbia)
cliff	la scogliera
shell	la conchiglia
pebbles	i ciottoli
rock	la roccia
little island	l'isola piccola
island	l'isola
jetty	l'imbarcadero
pier	il pontile
quay	la banchina
reef	la scogliera
surf	i cavalloni / la spuma
shore	la riva
coast	il litorale
estuary	l'estuario
cape	il capo
promontory	il promontorio
peninsula	la penisola

boats *imbarcazioni*

boat	la barca / il battello
rowing boat	la barca a remi
yacht	lo yacht
dinghy	il dinghy / canotto
motor boat	il motoscafo
steamer / waterbus	il vaporetto
ferry boat	il traghetto
car ferry	la nave-traghetto
cruiser	l'incrociatore
liner	il transatlantico

sailing *la navigazione a vela*

navigation	la navigazione
port	babordo
starboard	tribordo
buoy	la boa / il gavitello
light house	il faro
mast	l'albero
sail	la vela
rudder	il timone
anchor	l'ancora
satellite positioning	navigazione satellitare
automatic pilot	il pilota automatico
ropes	le cime / i cavi

the sea *il mare*

high tide	la marea alta
low tide	la marea bassa
sea-level	il livello del mare
calm	sereno / tranquillo
choppy	mosso / agitato
rough	grosso / tempestoso
sea floor	fondo marino
sandy	sabbioso
rocky	roccioso
rough	scabro
smooth	liscio

Useful verbs

to row	remare
to sail	navigare / veleggiare
to motor	navigare a motore
to tie up	ormeggiare
to anchor	ancorarsi
to cast off	levare gli ormeggi
to weigh anchor	levare l'ancora
to set sail	salpare

Useful phrases

When is high tide?	Quando è l'alta marea?
Where can I moor?	Dove posso ormeggiare?

8.4 Working in the countryside

Core vocabulary

agriculture	l'agricoltura
bee keeping	l'apicoltura
game keeper	il guardacaccia
horticulture	l'orticoltura
fruit growing	la frutticoltura
vine growing	la viticoltura
forestry	la selvicoltura
farm	la fattoria
market garden	l'orto (industriale)
farmhouse	la cascina / fattoria
barn	il granaio
stable / cattle shed	la stalla
stables (establishment)	la scuderia

cattle il bestiame

cows, heifer, bull, calf	le mucche, la giovenca, il toro, il vitello
sheep/ewe, ram, lamb	la pecora, l'ariete, l'agnello
pig, sow, boar, piglet	il maiale/porco, la scrofa, il verro, il porcellino
goats, nanny, billy, kid	le capre, la capra, il capro, il capretto
sheep/guard dog	il cane da pastore/da guardia
dog, bitch, puppy	il cane, la cagna, il cagnolino

poultry il pollame

hen	la gallina
chicken	il pollo
duck, duckling	l'anatra, l'anatroccolo
goose, gosling	l'oca, il papero
turkey	il tacchino
pheasant	il fagiano

crops il raccolto

cereals	i cereali
grain	il grano
barley	l'orzo
oats	l'avena
rice	il riso
rye	la segala

wheat	il frumento
hay	il fieno
straw	la paglia

farm jobs *lavori nella fattoria*

farmshop	il negozio di prodotti della fattoria
bee keeper	l'apicoltore
farmer	l'agricoltore / il coltivatore
farm worker / peasant	il contadino / il bracciante
horticulturalist	l'orticoltore
vet	il veterinario
vine grower	il viticoltore
vineyard	la vigna / il vigneto
vine	la vite
grapes	l'uva
cultivating	la coltivazione / la coltura
planting	piantare e seminare
spreading fertilizer	la fertilizzazione / concimazione
weeding	la diserbatura
harvesting	la mietitura / il raccolto
packaging	l'imballaggio

farm machinery *le macchine agricole*

tractor	il trattore
trailer	il rimorchio
plough	l'aratro
combine harvester	la mietitrebbia
harvester	la mietitrice

farm shop signs *cartelli nella fattoria*

fresh olive oil	olio d'oliva fresco
wine tasting	degustazione di vini
farmhouse cheese	formaggio di propria produzione
goat's cheese	formaggio di capra

Useful verbs

to feed	nutrire, dare da mangiare a
to milk	mungere
to raise / breed	allevare / far riprodurre
to sow	seminare
to fertilize	fertilizzare / concimare
to weed	diserbare

to pick	(rac)cogliere
to harvest	mietere / raccogliere
to take to market	portare al mercato

Useful phrases

Beware of the dog / bull!	Attenti al cane / toro!
Please shut the gate	Si prega di chiudere il cancello
electric fence	la recinzione elettrica
No entry	Vietato l'ingresso

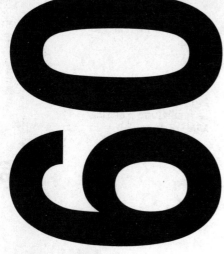

09 hobbies and sports

9.1 Hobbies

Core vocabulary

What do you like doing?	Che cosa ti piace fare?
I like ...	mi piace ...
acting	recitare
cooking	cucinare
dancing	ballare
modern	balli moderni
ballroom	il ballo liscio
DIY	il faidate
drawing	disegnare
gardening	fare giardinaggio
going for a walk	fare quattro passi
going out (socially)	uscire
horse riding	andare a cavallo
listening to music	ascoltare musica
meeting people	fare la conoscenza della gente
painting	dipingere / pitturare
photography	fotografare
playing tennis / football*	giocare a (tennis / calcio)
pottery	fare ceramica
reading	leggere
sailing	andare in barca a vela
sewing	cucire
singing	cantare
sport	fare sport
walking	camminare
watching films	guardare un film
watching television	guardare la televisione / la tivù
writing	scrivere

*See also p. 137.

outdoor pursuits *le attività all'aria aperta*

birdwatching	il bird-watching
fishing	pescare / la pesca
hunting	cacciare / la caccia
shooting	andare a caccia / tirare
rambling / hiking	fare escursioni a piedi
archaeology	l'archeologia
astronomy	l'astronomia
history	la storia
visiting historical sites	visitare i siti storici
touring	viaggiare / fare un giro

indoors *al coperto*

playing chess	giocare a scacchi
playing cards	giocare a carte
playing bridge	giocare a bridge
playing bingo	giocare a tombola
doing jigsaw puzzles	fare i puzzle
playing dominoes	giocare a domino
playing draughts	giocare a dama
billiards / snooker	giocare a biliardo
playing table football	giocare a calcetto
doing crosswords	fare i cruciverba

making music *fare musica*

playing in an orchestra	suonare in un'orchestra
singing in a group / a choir	cantare in un gruppo / un coro
playing an instrument	suonare uno strumento musicale
piano	il piano(forte)
guitar	la chitarra
violin	il violino
trumpet	la tromba
drums	la batteria

Useful verbs

to attend	assistere a / partecipare a
to be a member of	essere socio di
to be interested in	interessarsi di
to be keen on	essere appassionato di
to enjoy	piacere a (mi piace)
to enjoy oneself	divertirsi
to meet	incontrare / fare la conoscenza di
to spend my time	passare il tempo

Useful phrases

What do you do in your free-time?	Cosa fai / fa nel tempo libero?
Do you like ...?	Ti / Le piace ...?
I like meeting people	Mi piace trovarmi con altre persone
I do (painting)	Faccio (la pittura)
I belong to a club	Sono socio di un club
We meet every ...	Ci vediamo ogni ...

It's interesting	È interessante
It's fantastic	È fantastico
It's boring	È noioso
I *am interested in* ...	Mi interessa ...

9.2 Sports

ball games *giochi di pallone*

football	il calcio
footballer	il calciatore
ball	il pallone
team	la squadra
goal	il gol
match	la partita
football ground	il campo di calcio /
stadium	lo stadio
score	il punteggio / i punti
rugby	il rugby
player	il giocatore
pitch	il campo di rugby
to score a try	segnare una meta
basketball	la pallacanestro
basket	il canestro
volleyball	la pallavolo
net	la rete
hockey	l'hockey
hockey stick	il bastone da hockey
golf	il golf
golf club	la mazza da golf
golf course	il campo di golf
green	il green
hole	la buca
bunker	il bunker

racket games *i giochi di racchetta*

tennis	il tennis
tennis racquet / racket	la racchetta da tennis
tennis court	il campo da tennis
tennis ball	la palla da tennis
tennis player	il giocatore di tennis
badminton	il badminton
net	la rete
shuttlecock	il volano

squash	lo squash
squash court	il campo da squash
squash racquet	la racchetta da squash
(Italian) bowls	il gioco delle bocce

martial arts *le arti marziali*

boxing	il pugilato / la boxe
*judo**	il judo
*karate**	il karatè
*tae-kwando**	il tae-kwando
wrestling	la lotta libera

*Most of these sports keep the same name as in their country of origin.

non-team sports *gli sport individuali*

athletics	l'atletica
running	la corsa
cross country	il cross country / la corsa campestre
jumping	il salto / saltare
hurdles	la corsa a ostacoli
track	la pista
timekeeper	il cronometrista
gymnastics / keep fit	la ginnastica
aerobics	l'aerobica
jogging	il jogging
weight lifting	il sollevamento pesi
weight training	l'allenamento con i pesi
yoga	lo yoga

Useful verbs

to *win*	vincere
to *lose*	perdere
to *draw*	pareggiare
to *box*	fare il pugile
to *do*	fare
to *jog*	fare jogging
to *run*	correre

Football is, of course, the sport which arouses most passion across Italy, and the national team, **gli Azzurri** *the Blues*, consistently achieve high status in international competitions. The Italian league is among the most expensive and best in quality in the world; great teams such as Inter, Roma, Lazio, Juventus, AC Milan and Napoli are famous worldwide. Second to football in terms of national pride is **Formula 1** motor racing, with the red of Ferrari, with its prancing horse crest rivalling the blue football shirts for the top position among Italian icons. Cycling is another major national sport: cyclists compete for the **maglia rosa**, *the pink jersey*, in the **Giro d'Italia** and the **maglia gialla**, *the yellow jersey*, in the **Giro di Francia**.

9.3 More sports

water sports *gli sport acquatici*

canoeing	il canottaggio
canoe	la canoa
paddle	la pagaia
diving (deep sea)	il tuffo / l'immersione (a grande profondità)
wet suit	la muta (da subacqueo)
dry suit	la sottomuta
gas bottles	le bombole del gas
mask	la maschera
flippers	le pinne
snorkel	il boccaglio
rowing	il canottaggio
boat	la barca
oars	i remi
sailing	la vela
sail	la vela
surfing	il surf / surfing
surf board	la tavola da surf
waterskiing	lo sci acquatico
windsurfing	il windsurf
wind surfer	il windsurfista
yachting	la navigazione da diporto
yacht	lo yacht
dinghy	il dinghy / canotto
swimming	il nuoto
breast stroke	il nuoto a rana
front crawl	lo stilo libero / il crawl

butterfly	il nuoto a farfalla
backstroke	il dorso
diving	il tuffo / i tuffi
swimming pool	la piscina
length	la lunghezza
diving board	il trampolino
swimming costume	il costume da bagno
goggles	gli occhiali

other sports *altri sport*

archery	il tiro con l'arco
bow	l'arco
arrow	la freccia
target	il bersaglio
cycling	il ciclismo
racing bike	la bicicletta da corsa
mountain bike	la mountain bike
bike	la bicicletta
handlebars	il manubrio
saddle	la sella / il sellino
saddle bag	la borsa
fencing	la scherma
foil	il fioretto
horse riding	l'equitazione (f)
saddle	la sella
bridle	la briglia
stirrups	le staffe
rollerskating	il pattinaggio a rotelle
skates	i pattini a rotelle
skateboarding	fare lo skateboard
skateboard	lo skateboard
climbing / mountaineering	l'alpinismo
rock climbing	la roccia
potholing / caving	l'esplorazione speleologica
climbing boots	gli scarponi da montagna
rope	la corda / fune
karabiner	il moschettone
rucksack	lo zaino

winter sports *gli sport invernali*

skiing	lo sci
skis	gli sci
poles	i bastoni
piste	la pista

snowboarding	fare lo snowboard
snowboard	snowboard
sledging	andare in slitta
sledge	la slitta
toboganning	andare in slittino
toboggan	lo slittino
ice skating	il pattinaggio
skates	i pattini
ice rink	la pista di pattinaggio

Useful phrases

I enjoy doing ...	Mi piace molto fare ...
I am good at ...	Sono bravo in ...
I am not good at ...	Non sono bravo in ...

10

clothing

10.1 Garments and styles

ladies fashion *la moda femminile*

blouse	la blusa / camicetta
cardigan	il cardigan
dress	il vestito
evening dress	l'abito da sera
sun dress	il prendisole
jacket	la giacca
long jacket	la giacca lunga
short jacket	la giacca corta
jersey	la maglia
shorts	i calzoncini / gli shorts
skirt	la gonna
suit	l'abito
trouser suit	il completo pantalone
trousers	i pantaloni / calzoni
lingerie	la biancheria intima / lingerie
bra	il reggipetto / reggiseno
knickers	le mutandine
slip	la sottoveste
stockings	le calze
tights	il collant
nightie	la camicia da notte
pyjamas	il pigiama
negligee	il négligé / la vestaglia

men's fashion *la moda maschile*

blazer	il blazer
jacket	la giacca
dinner jacket	lo smoking
jeans	i jeans
jumper	il maglione
pullover	il pullover
shirt	la camicia
shorts	i calzoncini / gli shorts
socks	i calzini
suit	l'abito
sweatshirt	la felpa
T-shirt	la maglietta
tie	la cravatta
trousers	i pantaloni / calzoni
belt	la cintura
braces	le bretelle
waistcoat	il panciotto

boxer shorts	i calzoncini
underpants	lo slip / le mutande
vest	la maglia / la canottiera
pyjamas	il pigiama

outerwear *i vestiti per uscire*

coat	il cappotto / soprabito
raincoat	l'impermeabile
jacket	la giacca
hat	il cappello
scarf	la sciarpa
gloves	i guanti

Useful verbs

to wear	portare / indossare
to fit	andare bene (di misura)
to suit	stare bene

Useful phrases

I will be wearing …	porterò / indosserò …
a dark suit	un abito scuro
a coat and hat	un soprabito e un cappello
a sweatshirt, jeans and trainers	una felpa, i jeans e delle scarpe da ginnastica
What will you be wearing?	Che cosa porterai?
What size are you?	Che taglia porti / porta?
it is too short	è troppo corto
it is too wide	è troppo largo
it is too long	è troppo lungo
it is too tight	è troppo stretto
Have you got anything bigger/smaller?	Ha qualcosa di più grande?
in a different colour?	in un colore diverso?
it suits you / it doesn't suit you	le sta bene / non le sta bene

10.2 The garment

measurements *le misure*

tape measure	il metro a nastro
length	la lunghezza
width	la larghezza
size	la taglia

parts of the garment *parti dell'indumento*

collar	il collo / colletto
neck	il collo
shoulders	le spalle
sleeves	le maniche
chest	il petto
waist	la vita
cuffs	i polsini

materials *le stoffe*

fabric	la stoffa
it is made in ...	è fatto di ...
cotton	il cotone
fur	la pelliccia
artificial fur	la pelliccia artificiale
jersey	il jersey
leather	il cuoio
linen	(la tela di) lino
satin	il raso / satin
silk	la seta
suede	la pelle scamosciata
synthetic fibre	la fibra sintetica
tweed	il tweed
velvet	il velluto
wool	la lana

patterns *motivi*

it is	è ...
floral	a fiori
folded	piegato
multi-colour	multicolore
patterned	a disegni
pleated	a pieghe
plain (one colour)	in tinta unica
self-coloured	monocromatico
spotted	a pallini
striped	a righe / strisce

repairs *riparazioni*

button	il bottone
cotton	il filo
fastener	la chiusura / il fermaglio
needle	l'ago
thimble	il ditale
ribbon	il nastro

scissors   le forbici
sewing machine   la macchina da cucire
velcro   il velcro
zip   la cerniera (lampo) / lo zip

washing *lavaggio*

detergent   il detersivo / detergente
detergent for wool   il detersivo per lana
fabric softener   l'ammorbidente
soap powder   il detersivo in polvere

Useful verbs

to wash   lavare
to dry   asciugare
to dry clean   lavare a secco
to iron   stirare
to mend   rammendare

Useful phrases

I have lost a button   Ho perso un bottone
Can I get this laundered /   Posso far lavare / far
  dry cleaned / pressed   lavare a secco / far
  (ironed)?   stirare questo?
How long will it take?   Quanto tempo ci vuole
                                    per farlo?

Can you remove this stain?   Può smacchiare questo?
Can you sew this button on?   Può attaccare questo
                                    bottone?

Can you take it in?   Lo/la può stringere?
Can you shorten it?   Lo/la può accorciare?

This garment must be   Pulire a secco
  dry cleaned
This garment can be   Lavabile in lavatrice
  machine washed
Handwash only   Lavare solo a mano
Don't use bleach   Non usare decolorante

10.3 Special occasions

going to work *al lavoro*

uniform	l'uniforme (f)
apron	il grembiule
overall	il camice

It's raining! *Piove!*

rain coat	l'impermeabile
rain hat	il cappello impermeabile
waterproof trousers	i pantaloni impermeabili
rubber boots	gli stivali di gomma
umbrella	l'ombrello

It's cold! *Fa freddo!*

anorak	la giacca a vento
walking boots	gli scarponi da montagna
thick socks	i calzettoni
woolly hat	il cappello di lana
gloves	i guanti

on the beach *sulla spiaggia*

swimming costume	il costume da bagno
bikini	il bikini
trunks	i calzoncini da bagno
flippers	le pinne
goggles	la maschera / gli occhiali
snorkel	il boccaglio
flip flops	gli infradito
sun tan cream	la crema solare

a night on the town *una bella serata fuori*

evening dress	l'abito da sera
high heels	i tacchi alti
smart clothes	i vestiti eleganti

playing a game *fare una partita*

baseball hat	il cappello di baseball
polo shirt	la polo
shorts	i calzoncini
socks	i calzini
trainers	le scarpe da ginnastica
sweatshirt	la felpa
T-shirt	la maglietta

for a party *per una festa*
   formal dress   l'abito da cerimonia
   casual dress   il (vestito) casual

jewellery *i gioielli*
   bracelet   il braccialetto
   brooch   la spilla
   earrings   gli orecchini
   necklace   la collana
   ring   l'anello
   watch   l'orologio

   silver   l'argento
   gold   l'oro
   platinum   il platino
   diamond   il diamante
   emerald   lo smeraldo
   ruby   il rubino
   sapphire   lo zaffiro
   semi-precious stone   la pietra semipreziosa

Useful verbs
   to wear   portare

Useful phrases
   He/she always looks   Ha sempre un aspetto …
     casual   casual
     fashionable   alla moda
     smart   elegante
     unfashionable   fuori moda
     untidy   disordinato

10.4 Footwear

Core vocabulary
   the shoe shop   il negozio di calzature / scarpe
   hosiery   il reparto calze e calzini
   socks   i calzini
   stockings   le calze
   tights   il collant
   leggings   i pantacollant / fuseaux

I would like a pair of ...	vorrei un paio di ...
boots	stivali
clogs	zoccoli
flip flops	infradito
moccasin	moccassini
sandals	sandali
shoes	scarpe
slip-ons	scarpe senza allacciatura
slippers	pantofole / ciabatte
tennis shoes	scarpe da tennis
trainers	scarpe da ginnastica
wellingtons / rubber boots	stivaloni di gomma
ballet shoes	le scarpe da balletto
climbing boots	gli scarponi da alpinismo
cycling shoes	le scarpe da ciclismo
dancing shoes	le scarpe da ballo
diving boots	le scarpe da tuffatore
flippers	le pinne
ski boots	gli scarponi da sci
snowboard boots	gli scarponi da snowboard
steel tipped boots	gli scarponi / stivali a puntali di acciaio
walking boots	gli scarponi da montagna
leather	il cuoio
rubber	la gomma
synthetics	le fibre sintetiche
high-heeled shoes	le scarpe a tacchi alti
flat shoes	le scarpe a tacchi bassi
shoe polish	il lucido da scarpe
shoe cleaner	la spazzole / lo strofinaccio per le scarpe
shoe protector	il liquido impermeabilizzante per scarpe
shoe stretcher	la forma (per scarpe)
chiropody	la chiropodia
massage	il massaggio
reflexology	la riflessologia
foot	il piede
toe	il dito del piede
ankle	la caviglia
sole	la pianta del piede

| toe nails | le unghie del piede |
| arch of the foot | l'arco plantare |

Useful verbs

to try shoes on	provare le scarpe
to put on your shoes	mettersi le scarpe
to take off your shoes	togliersi le scarpe
to get blisters	farsi venire le vesciche

Useful phrases

bare foot	a piedi scalzi / nudi
I have got sore feet	Mi fanno male i piedi
I have got blisters	Ho le vesciche
Have you got a plaster?	Ha un cerotto?
Please remove your shoes in the house	Per favore, togliti le scarpe quando sei in casa
What shoe size are you?	Che numero di scarpe porti / porta?
These shoes are comfortable / uncomfortable	Queste scarpe sono comode / scomode

11

travel

11.1 Travel

Core vocabulary

journey	il viaggio
itinerary	l'itinerario
route	l'itinerario / il percorso
map	la mappa / cartina
overland	per (via di) terra
by air / plane	in aereo
by sea	per mare
by rail / train	in treno
by coach	in pullman
by car	in macchina
by hire car	in macchina a noleggio
by boat	in barca / in nave
by ferry	in traghetto
by bike	in bicicletta
on horseback	a cavallo
on foot	a piedi
timetable	l'orario
ticket	il biglietto
booking, reservation	la prenotazione
on-line booking	la prenotazione per internet / on-line
arrival	l'arrivo
departure	la partenza

Useful verbs

to travel	viaggiare
to go	andare
to sail	navigare / viaggiare per mare
to fly	volare / andare in aereo
to drive	viaggiare in macchina
to tour	fare un giro di / fare un viaggio in
to arrive	arrivare
to leave	partire

Useful phrases

Can you help me, please?	Mi può aiutare?/ Mi aiuti, per favore!

I'm lost	Mi sono perso
How do I get to …?	Come posso andare a …?
What is the best way to go to …?	Mi sa indicare la strada migliore per …?
Is it far?	È lontano?
How far is it?	Quanto è lontano?
How long does it take?	Quanto tempo ci vuole per andare?

▌ Expand your vocabulary by grouping words which have the same root: **viaggio** means *journey*; **viaggiare** *to travel*; **agenzia di viaggi** *travel agency*.

11.2 Travel by train

Core vocabulary

station	la stazione
station master	il capostazione
booking office	la biglietteria / l'ufficio prenotazioni
ticket machine	la biglietteria automatica
timetable	l'orario
ticket	il biglietto
single ticket	il biglietto di andata
return ticket	il biglietto di andata e ritorno

▌ Train travel in Italy is very reasonably priced, and trains are very punctual; among other express trains are the various **Intercity** trains, **Pendolino** and **Eurostar**.

types of ticket	tipi di biglietto
child	per bambino
adult	per adulto
family	offerta famiglie
senior/pensioners	per pensionati
group	di gruppo
arrivals	arrivi
departures	partenze
indicator board	il tabellone
information	informazioni (f pl)
waiting room	la sala d'attesa
platform	il marciapiede / binario
subway	il sottopassaggio

stairs	la scala
lift	l'ascensore (m)
train	il treno
express	l'espresso
Inter-city	l'intercity (m)
local / slow	il treno locale
underground	il metrò / la metropolitana
coach	la carrozza / vettura
non-smoking	per non fumatori
first class	di prima classe
buffet	il servizio ristoro
personnel	il personale
guard	il capotreno
ticket inspector	il controllore
train driver	il macchinista
passenger	il passeggero
traveller	il viaggiatore
level crossing	il passaggio a livello
railway track	la linea ferroviaria
signals	i segnali ferroviari
luggage	i bagagli
suitcase	la valigia
left luggage	il deposito bagagli

Useful verbs

to book a ticket	prenotare un biglietto
to make a reservation	fare una prenotazione

Useful phrases

Do I have to change?	Devo cambiare?
Is the train on time?	Il treno è / arriverà in orario?
How late is the train?	Con quanto ritardo arriva il treno?
Will I miss the connection?	Perderò la coincidenza?
Is there a car park at the station?	C'è un parcheggio alla stazione?
Which platform does it leave from?	Da quale binario parte il treno?
Is this the train for …?	È il treno per …?
This is my place	Questo posto è mio
I have a reservation	Ho fatto una prenotazione

the underground / subway	il metrò / la metropolitana
the line	la linea
How often does it run?	Ogni quanto c'è il treno?
Which line do I need for ...?	Quale linea devo prendere per ...?

11.3 Travel by plane

Core vocabulary

at the airport *all'aeroporto*

car park	il parcheggio
departures	le partenze
check-in desk	il check-in / banco accettazioni
luggage search	il controllo bagagli
security check	il controllo di sicurezza
Which class?	Quale classe?
economy	classe turistica
business	classe business
first	prima classe
ticket	il biglietto
passport	il passaporto
visa	il visto
green card	la carta verde
departure lounge	la sala partenze
executive lounge	la sala VIP
information	le informazioni (f)
announcements	gli annunci
flight	il volo
gate	l'uscita
delay	il ritardo

on the plane *in aereo*

row	la fila
seat	il posto
window seat	il posto vicino al finestrino
aisle seat	il posto vicino al corridoio
seat belt	la cintura di sicurezza
life jacket	il giubbotto di salvataggio
emergency exit	l'uscita di sicurezza
overhead locker	lo scomparto del bagaglio a mano
toilet	il gabinetto

pilot	il pilota
steward	lo steward
stewardess	la hostess
Can I have ...?	Mi dia ...
earphones	la cuffia
a blanket	una coperta
a pillow	un cuscino
a glass of water	un bicchiere d'acqua

landing *l'atterraggio*

arrivals	arrivi
baggage reclaim	il ritiro bagagli
customs	la dogana
duty	il dazio

Useful verbs

to leave / depart	partire
to take off	decollare
to fly	volare
to land	atterrare
to arrive	arrivare
to navigate	navigare
to put the seat back	inclinare il sedile indietro
to put the seat upright	mettere il sedile in posizione verticale
to stow the table	chiudere il tavolino pieghevole
to experience turbulence	attraversare una zona di turbolenza dell'aria

Useful phrases

The plane is delayed	L'aereo è in ritardo
Your flight leaves from gate ...	Il suo volo parte dall'uscita numero ...
Please will you return to your seats and fasten your seat-belts	Si prega di tornare ai propri posti e allacciare la cintura di sicurezza
We are flying at an altitude of ... and a speed of ...	Siamo a un'altezza di ... e a una velocità di ...
My luggage is missing	I miei bagagli non ci sono

11.4 Travel by car

Core vocabulary

car	la macchina
estate car	la station waggon / l'auto modello familiare
four wheel drive	con trazione a quattro ruote motrici
sports car	l'automobile sportiva
convertible	l'auto decappottabile
automatic	l'automobile con cambio automatico
2/4 doors	con 2/4 portiere
16 valves	con 16 valvole
the pedals	i pedali
accelerator	l'acceleratore (m)
brake	il freno
clutch	il pedale della frizione
the windscreen	il parabrezza
the gears	le marce
the gear lever	la leva del cambio
the steering wheel	il volante
the handbrake	il freno a mano
the indicators	le frecce
the lights	le luci
headlamps	i fari / fanali
side lights	le luci di posizione
on full	con gli abbaglianti accesi
on dipped	con i fari abbassati / gli anabbaglianti
the speedometer	il tachimetro
the mileometer	il contachilometri
the petrol gauge	la spia della benzina

the interior l'interno

seats	i sedili
safety belt	la cintura di sicurezza
leg room	lo spazio per le gambe
glove compartment	il vano portaoggetti
sunvisor	l'aletta parasole
wing mirror	lo specchietto laterale esterno
rearview mirror	lo specchietto retrovisore
heating	il riscaldamento
air conditioning	l'aria condizionata

the wheels *le ruote*

tyres	le gomme / i pneumatici
valve	la valvola
tyre pressure	la pressione dei pneumatici
jack	il cric
spare wheel	la ruota di scorta

the exterior *l'esterno*

boot	il bagagliaio
bumper	il paraurti
number plate	la targa
fog lights	i fari antinebbia
rear lights	le luci posteriori
exhaust	il tubo di scappamento
battery	la batteria
radiator	il radiatore

getting technical *aspetti tecnici*

ignition	l'accensione (f)
spark plug	la candela
water hose	il manicotto dell'acqua
oil pressure	la pressione dell'olio
fan belt	la cinghia della ventola
windscreen wiper	il tergicristallo
windscreen washer	il lavacristallo
warning light	la spia luminosa

Useful verbs

to drive	guidare
to put your lights on	accendere le luci
to turn your lights off	spegnere le luci
to put your indicator on	mettere la freccia / segnalare
to give way	dare la precedenza
to overtake	sorpassare

Useful phrases

You have left your lights on	Ha lasciato le luci accese
How do I move the seat?	Come posso aggiustare il sedile?

11.5 The road

Core vocabulary

a country road	una strada di campagna
a main road	una strada principale
a one-way road	una strada a senso unico
a dual carriageway	una strada a doppia carreggiata
a motorway	un'autostrada
a motorway lane	una corsia dell'autostrada
the inside lane	la corsia di destra
the outside lane	la corsia di sinistra
the central reservation	la banchina spartitraffico
the access road	la strada d'accesso
motorway access road	il raccordo di entrata

Most, but not all motorways in Italy are toll roads. It is a good idea to have enough change ready when you get to a **casello** *toll station*, though you can also pay with a credit card or by **telepass**, an electronic system which reads your number plate and charges the toll directly to your account.

the road surface is …	il fondo stradale è
good/bad	in buone / cattive condizioni
smooth/uneven	liscio / disuguale
bumpy	dissestato
with potholes	con buche
the intersection / cross-roads	l'incrocio
T-junction	l'incrocio a T
the roundabout	la rotatoria
the bridge	il ponte
the toll bridge	il ponte a pedaggio
the level crossing	il passaggio a livello
traffic lights	il semaforo

Note that Italian traffic lights go from green (**luce verde**) to amber (**luce gialla**) to red (**luce rossa**), then straight back to green with no red+amber phase.

road works	i lavori stradali
emergency traffic lights	il semaforo d'emergenza
the diversion	la deviazione
road signs	i cartelli stradali
crawler lane	la corsia riservata al traffico lento

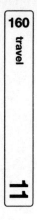

hard shoulder	la corsia d'emergenza
the speed limit	il limite di velocità
the speed camera	il controllo elettronico di velocità
traffic police	la polizia stradale
driving licence	la patente di guida
insurance	l'assicurazione
fine	la multa
garage (for repairs / service)	l'autofficina
petrol station	la stazione di servizio / il benzinaio
petrol	la benzina
diesel	il diesel
air	l'aria
water	l'acqua
oil	l'olio
oil change	il cambio dell'olio
emergency services	i servizi di pronto intervento
breakdown	il guasto

Useful verbs

to speed	andare a velocità eccessiva
to accelerate	accelerare
to slow down	rallentare
to brake	frenare
to break down	avere un guasto

Useful phrases

I have broken down	La mia macchina è guasta
The car is overheating	La macchina si surriscalda
The engine has stopped	Il motore non funziona più / si è fermato
I have a puncture	Ho forato una gomma / Ho una gomma a terra
The silencer has blown	La marmitta è scoppiata

12

tourism

12.1 Where to go

Core vocabulary

the tourism industry	l'industria turistica, il turismo
travel agency	l'agenzia di viaggi
a brochure	un opusculo / dépliant
the tourist	il/la turista
an excursion	un'escursione, una gita
a tour	un giro
a coach trip	un'escursione in pullman
a guided visit	una visita guidata
a cruise	una crociera
holiday resort	il luogo di villeggiatura
seaside	la spiaggia / il mare
sea sand and sun	il mare, la sabbia e il sole
mountains and lakes	le montagne e i laghi
countryside	la campagna
adventure holidays	le vacanze di avventure
winter sports	gli sport invernali
outdoor pursuits	le attività all'aperto
to go on holiday	andare in vacanza / prendere le ferie
to go on summer holiday	prendere le vacanze estive
national holiday	le feste civili

i Expand your vocabulary by grouping words which have the same root, e.g. **turista**, **turismo** and **turistico**.

12.2 What to take

Core vocabulary

luggage	i bagagli
suitcase	la valigia
travel bag	la borsa da viaggio
overnight bag	la borsa da viaggio / la ventiquattrore
rucksack	lo zaino
hand luggage	il bagaglio a mano
passport	il passaporto
visa	il visto
tickets	i biglietti

insurance	l'assicurazione
driving licence	la patente di guida
credit card	la carta di credito
currency	la valuta estera
traveller's cheque	il traveller's cheque
emergency phone number	il numero di telefono d'emergenza
laptop	il laptop
mobile phone	il telefonino
sponge bag	il nécessaire
toilet bag	il nécessaire da toilette
soap	il sapone
toothbrush	lo spazzolino da denti
toothpaste	il dentifricio
razor	il rasoio
electric razor	il rasoio elettrico
nail scissors	le forbicine per le unghie
tweezers	le pinzette
shampoo	lo shampoo
conditioner	il balsamo
hairbrush	la spazzola per capelli
comb	il pettine
face cream	la crema per il viso
hand cream	la crema per le mani
cleanser	il detergente
moisturizer	il prodotto idratante
sun cream	la crema solare
waterproof sun cream	la crema solare impermeabile
after sun cream	la crema doposole
factor 10	la crema solare con fattore di protezione 10

Useful verbs

to pack	fare le valigie / i bagagli
to unpack	disfare le valigie / i bagagli
to fold	piegare
to hang up	appendere
to wash	lavare
to dry clean	lavare a secco
to mend	rammendare / aggiustare / riparare
to press / iron	stirare

Useful phrases

I have lost my luggage	Ho perso i miei bagagli
I can't find …	Non trovo …
Have you got a …?	Ha un(a) …?
Where can I get a …?	Dove posso trovare un(a) …?
Where is the nearest …?	Dove sta il/la …. più vicino?

12.3 Where to stay

accommodation	l'alloggio
two-star hotel	un albergo a due stelle
three-star hotel	un albergo a tre stelle
luxury hotel	un albergo di lusso
inn	la locanda
bed and breakfast	la pensione familiare
holiday house / home	la casa di villeggiatura
youth hostel	l'ostello della gioventù
camp site	il campeggio
caravan site	il campeggio per roulotte
the entrance	l'entrata / l'ingresso
the reception	la reception
the night porter	il portiere di notte
the manager	il direttore / gerente
the staff	il personale
the porter	il portiere
a single room	una camera singola
a room with double bed	una (camera) matrimoniale
a twin bedded room	una (camera) doppia
a family room	una camera familiare
with shower	con doccia
with bathroom	con bagno
with toilet	con gabinetto
with phone	con telefono
with television	con televisione
with Internet connection	con connessione a Internet
with a balcony	con balcone
with a sea view	con vista sul mare
with air conditioning	con aria condizionata
reception	la reception
stairs	la scala

lift	l'ascensore
restaurant	il ristorante
fitness room	la palestra per esercizi di fitness
pool	la piscina
hot tub	la vasca per idromassaggio
the bill	il conto

Useful phrases

Have you got anything ...?	Ha qualcosa di ...?
bigger / smaller	più grande / piccolo
cheaper / better	meno caro / migliore
quieter	più tranquillo
a non-smoking room	una camera per non fumatori
It is too noisy	È troppo rumoroso
The shower doesn't work	Non funziona la doccia
There is no hot water	Non c'è acqua calda
There is no plug in the sink	Non c'è il tappo nel lavandino
Can I have another towel?	Posso avere un altro asciugamano?
more coat hangers?	altre grucce?
the iron?	il ferro da stiro?

12.4 Camping and caravanning

Core vocabulary

camp site	il campeggio
caravan	la roulotte
camper van	il camper
trailer	il rimorchio
tent	la tenda
frame tent	la tenda familiare
site	il posto
a flat site	un posto piano
a shady site	un posto ombreggiato
facilities	le attrezzature
electricity	l'elettricità / la corrente
water	l'acqua
running water	l'acqua corrente
drinking water	l'acqua potabile
water tap	il rubinetto dell'acqua
power socket	la presa di corrente

washrooms / toilets	i gabinetti
showers	le docce
washbasins	i lavandini
hairdryers	gli asciugacapelli
cooking area	la cucina
gas rings	i fornelli a gas
washing up sinks	i lavelli
washing machines	le lavatrici
clothes driers	le asciugatrici / asciugabiancheria
drying area	la zona per asciugare i panni
restaurant	il ristorante
bar	il bar
shop	il negozio
swimming pool	la piscina
paddling pool	la piscina per bambini
children's play area	il campo giochi per bambini
swings	l'altalena
slide	lo scivolo
roundabout	la giostra
tent	la tenda
tent pegs	i picchetti (da tenda)
tent pole	il palo da tenda
guy ropes	i tiranti / cavi
ground-sheet	il telone impermeabile
sleeping bag	il sacco a pelo
torch	la torcia elettrica
blanket	la coperta
gas cooker	la cucina a gas
gas bottle	la bombola del gas

Useful verbs

to tow	rimorchiare
to park	parcheggiare
to put up	montare
to take down	smontare
to hook up (connect)	collegare
to get wet	bagnarsi
to wash / do the washing	fare il bucato
to dry	asciugare

Useful phrases

Can you help me?	Mi può aiutare?

I don't understand how the ... works	Non capisco come funziona il/la ...
Where is the ...?	Dove sta il/la ...?
Is there electricity / water / shade?	C'è elettricità /acqua / ombra?
Do you have ...?	Ha ...?
When is the shop open?	A che ora apre il negozio?
Where can I get ...?	Dove posso trovare ...?

12.5 What are you going to do?

Core vocabulary

an activity holiday	delle vacanze con attività programmate
we want to go ...	vogliamo andare a fare ...
swimming	il nuoto
diving	i tuffi
water skiing	lo sci nautico
surfing	il surf
walking	la camminata
hiking	la gita a piedi
climbing	l'alpinismo
gliding	il volo a vela
paragliding	il volo col paracadute
hanggliding	il volo col deltaplano
do sport	fare dello sport
play tennis	giocare a tennis
play volleyball	giocare a pallavolo
go bike riding	fare ciclismo
we want to see	vogliamo vedere
monuments / sights	i monumenti
castles	i castelli
archeological sites	i siti archeologici
ancient monuments	i monumenti antichi
historic buildings	gli edifici storici
the scenery	il paesaggio
animals	gli animali
we want ...	vogliamo ...
to have a good time	divertirci*
to have a rest	riposarci*
to relax	rilassarci*

sun, sea and sand	sole, mare e sabbia
to do nothing	non fare niente
to be waited on	essere serviti

i These expressions are reflexive, and we have put the pronoun into the **ci** form, which is what you will need after **vogliamo**.

In winter I like to go ...	d'inverno mi piace ...
skiing	andare a sciare
snowboarding	fare lo snowboard
sledging	andare in slitta
ice skating	fare il pattinaggio sul ghiaccio
to find some sun	trovare il sole

Useful phrases

What is there to see / do?	Che c'è da vedere / fare?
Is it suitable for ...?	È adatto per ...?
older people	gli anziani
younger people	i giovani
children	i bambini

12.6 On the beach

Core vocabulary

sea	il mare
coast	la costa
beach	la spiaggia
bay	la baia
shore	la riva
sand	la sabbia
rocks	le rocce
rock pools	le pozze d'acqua
sea shells	le conchiglie
tide	la marea
waves	le onde

private / public beach	la spiaggia privata / pubblica
wind break	il frangivento
shelter	il rifugio
parasol	il parasole
lounger	il lettino da spiaggia
deck chair	la sedia a sdraio
air mattress	il materassino gonfiabile
shower	la doccia

towel	l'asciugamano	
swimming costume	il costume da bagno	
trunks	i calzoncini da bagno	
bikini	il bikini	
suntan lotion	l'olio solare	
total screen / sunblock	il filtro solare	
sun glasses	gli occhiali da sole	
rubber ring	la ciambella	
arm bands	i braccioli per bambini	
sandcastle	il castello di sabbia	
bucket	il secchio	
spade	la paletta	
kite	l'aquilone	
snorkel	il respiratore subacqueo / boccaglio	
flippers	le pinne	
wet suit	la muta da subacqueo	
dry suit	la sottomuta	
inflatable	gonfiabile	
hand/foot pump	la pompa a mano / a pedale	
surf board	il surf	
wind surfer	il windsurfista	
jetski	la moto acquatica	
waterski	lo sci nautico	
fish	il pesce	
shells	le conchiglie	
octopus	il polpo	
squid	il calamaro	
mussels	le cozze	
scallops	le cappe sante	
shrimps	i gamberetti	
jelly fish	la medusa	

Useful verbs

to snorkel	nuotare con il boccaglio
to sunbathe	prendere il sole
to relax	rilassarsi
to play	giocare
to dig	scavare
to dive	tuffarsi
to sting	pizzicare / pungere
to waterski	praticare lo sci nautico

Useful phrases

The tide is in / out	La marea è alta / bassa
It is safe for bathing / swimming	Non è pericoloso bagnarsi / nuotare
I have been stung by a jelly fish	Mi ha pizzicato una medusa
He/She is out of her depth	Lui/Lei non tocca
He/She can't swim	Lui/Lei non sa nuotare
He/She needs help	Ha bisogno di aiuto
Help!	Aiuto!

12.7 At sea

Core vocabulary

canoe	la canoa
jetski	la moto acquatica
motor boat	il motoscafo
outboard (motor)	il (motore) fuoribordo
RIB (rigid inflatable boat)	il gommone a chiglia rigida
rubber dinghy	il gommone
rowing boat	la barca a remi
sailing dinghy	la deriva
surf board	il surf
waterski	lo sci nautico
windsurfer	il windsurfista
yacht	il panfilo da diporto
emergency services	i servizi di pronto intervento
MAYDAY	MAYDAY
SOS	SOS
lifeboat (from shore)	la lancia di salvataggio
lifeboat (from ship)	la scialuppa di salvataggio
life jacket	il giubbotto di salvataggio
lifeguard	il bagnino
flare	il segnale luminoso
weather forecast	le previsioni del tempo
the sea is	il mare è
calm	calmo
rough	mosso
wind force	la forza del vento
gale force wind	il vento di bufera
rain	la pioggia
poor / good visibility	poca / buona visibilità
fog	la nebbia
equipment	l'attrezzatura

compass	la bussola
GPS (global satellite positioning)	il navigatore GPS
sails	le vele
hull	lo scafo
cabin	la cabina
berth	la cuccetta
wheel	il timone
harbour	il porto
port	il porto
lighthouse	il faro
port	(a) babordo
starboard	(a) tribordo
mooring	l'ormeggio
buoy	la boa
chain	la catena
anchor	l'ancora

Useful verbs

to sail	navigare
to navigate	navigare
to steer	governare / dirigere
to tie up / moor	ormeggiare
to anchor	ancorare
to rescue	salvare
to be rescued	essere salvato/a

12.8 The great outdoors

Core vocabulary

rucksack	lo zaino
sleeping bag	il sacco a pelo
ground mat / mattress	il materassino
torch	la torcia elettrica
penknife	il temperino
compass	la bussola
map	la mappa
water bottle	la borraccia
camping stove	il fornelletto a gas
matches	i fiammiferi
lighter	l'accendino
gas container	la bombola del gas
billycan (for cooking on stove)	il pentolino

bowl	la scodella / coppetta
knife / fork / spoon	il coltello / la forchetta / il cucchiaio
plate	il piatto
mug	il tazzone
emergency rations	le razioni di riserva
dried food	alimenti liofilizzati / disidratati
dried fruit	la frutta secca
nuts	le noci, le nocciole, le mandorle
chocolate	il cioccolato
transceiver (for snow rescue)	il ricetrasmettitore
mobile phone	il telefonino
batteries	le pile / la batteria
charger	il carica-batterie
plug	la spina
waterproofs	gli indumenti impermeabili
spare clothing	i vestiti di scorta
rope	la corda
climbing harness	l'imbracatura da alpinismo
climbing gear	l'attrezzatura da alpinismo
crampons	i ramponi
boots	gli stivali
ice axe	la piccozza da ghiaccio

Useful phrases

I have got … sore feet	Mi fanno male … i piedi
Have you got …	Hai / ha …?
spare socks	dei calzini di scorta
blisters	le vesciche
plasters	dei cerotti
antiseptic cream	della pomata antisettica
insect repellent	l'insettifugo
anti-histamine cream (for insect bites)	la crema antistaminica
Have you got something for …	Ha qualche cosa per …?
I have been stung by a wasp / bee	Mi ha punto una vespa / un'ape
I have been bitten by …	Mi ha morso …
a mosquito	una zanzara
a snake	un serpente
a dog	un cane

13

body and health

13.1 The face

Core vocabulary

head	la testa
face	la faccia / il viso
hair	i capelli
forehead	la fronte
ears	le orecchie
eyes	gli occhi
eyebrows	le sopracciglia
eyelashes	le ciglia
nose	il naso
nostrils	le narici
cheeks	le guance
chin	il mento
mouth	la bocca
lips	le labbra
tongue	la lingua
teeth	i denti
neck	il collo

He has a beard	ha la barba
a moustache	i baffi
He / she wears glasses	porta gli occhiali
contact lenses	le lenti a contatto
I am short/long-sighted	sono miope / presbite

toiletries *articoli di toeletta*

shampoo	lo shampoo
conditioner	il balsamo
face cream	la crema per il viso
moisturizer	la crema idratante
face pack	la maschera di bellezza
lip salve	il burro di cacao
shaving cream	la crema da barba
shaving brush	il pennello da barba
razor	il rasoio
electric razor	il rasoio elettrico
after shave lotion	il dopobarba
make-up	i cosmetici
mascara	il mascara
lipstick	il rossetto
eye shadow	l'ombretto
powder	la cipria

Useful verbs

to feel	sentire
to hear	sentire / udire
to see	vedere
to smell	sentire odore di
to taste	gustare / sentire il sapore di
to wink	fare l'occhiolino
to sleep	dormire
to smile	sorridere
to laugh	ridere
to talk	parlare
to shout	gridare
to cry	piangere
to snore	russare
to hiccup	avere il singhiozzo
to cough	tossire

Useful phrases

to have a facial	farsi fare un trattamento di bellezza per il viso
to have your hair done	andare dal parrucchiere
to have a nose job	essere operato al naso
to have plastic surgery	subire la chirurgia plastica
to have wrinkles	avere le rughe
to have a nice smile	avere un bel sorriso

13.2 The body

Core vocabulary

body	il corpo
shoulders	le spalle
back	la schiena
arms	le braccia
elbows	i gomiti
wrist	il polso
hands	le mani
fingers	le dita
thumb	il pollice
fingernails	le unghie

front	il davanti
side	il fianco
chest	il petto
breasts	i seni
nipples	i capezzoli
waist	la vita
hips	i fianchi
abdomen	l'addome
bottom	il sedere
sexual organs	gli organi sessuali
penis	il pene
balls	i coglioni
vagina	la vagina
legs	le gambe
thighs	le cosce
knees	le ginocchia
calves	i polpacci
ankle	la caviglia
foot	il piede
toes	le dita del piede
arch	l'arco
heel	il tallone
internal organs	gli organi interni
brain	il cervello
stomach	lo stomaco
belly	la pancia
throat	la gola
lungs	i polmoni
kidneys	i reni
heart	il cuore
blood	il sangue
veins	le vene
arteries	le arterie
a blood transfusion	una trasfusione di sangue
a blood donor	un donatore di sangue
my blood type	il mio gruppo sanguigno
intestines	gli intestini
skeleton	lo scheletro
bones	le ossa
joints	le articolazioni
nervous system	il sistema nervoso
nerves	i nervi
circulation	la circolazione

breathing	la respirazione
digestion	la digestione

Useful verbs

to feel	sentire
to touch	toccare
to stroke	accarezzare
to massage	massaggiare
to hold	tenere
to embrace	abbracciarsi
to kiss	baciarsi
to make love	fare l'amore
to kick	dar calci (a)
to walk	camminare
to run	correre
to jump	saltare

13.3 I need a doctor

Core vocabulary

doctor	il medico / dottore
appointment	l'appuntamento
surgery	l'ambulatorio
I have a pain ...	ho mal di ...
it hurts / they hurt	mi fa male / mi fanno male
I don't feel well	non mi sento bene
I can't sleep / eat / walk ...	non posso dormire / mangiare / camminare
I want to go to the toilet	voglio andare al gabinetto / al bagno
I feel sick	mi sento male / ho la nausea
I feel dizzy	mi gira la testa
I have got spots	ho dei foruncoli
I have been bitten / stung	sono stato morsicato / punto
I have a headache	ho mal di testa
toothache	mal di denti
earache	mal d'orecchi
a nose bleed	un'emorragia nasale
my eyes are sore	mi fanno male gli occhi

I *have stomach-ache*	ho mal di stomaco
heart burn	il bruciore di stomaco
indigestion	l'indigestione
high/low blood pressure	la pressione alta/bassa
my foot / hand / leg hurts	mi fa male il piede / la mano / la gamba

ailments *disturbi e malattie*

a cold	un raffreddore
flu (influenza)	l'influenza
measles	il morbillo
mumps	gli orecchioni
German measles	la rosolia
tonsillitis	la tonsillite
a cough	una tosse
sore throat	un mal di gola
indigestion	la cattiva digestione / l'indigestione
hypertension	l'ipertensione
constipation	la stitichezza
diarrhoea	la diarrea
polio	la polio(mielite)
hepatitis	l'epatite (f)
rabies	la rabbia / l'idrofobia
typhoid	la febbre tifoidea
cholera	il colera
yellow fever	la febbre gialla
malaria	la malaria
cancer	il cancro
multiple sclerosis	la sclerosi a placche
I *am allergic to*	sono allergico
penicillin	alla penicillina
nuts	alle noci
animals	agli animali
I *have hay fever*	ho il raffreddore da fieno
asthma	l'asma
He needs an inhaler	Lui ha bisogno di un inalatore
She is handicapped	Lei è handicappata
paraplegic	paraplegico
She has her period	Lei ha le mestruazioni

treatment *cure*

an injection / a jab for	un'iniezione per
immunization	l'immunizzazione
innoculation	l'inoculazione
medicine	la medicina
pills	le pillole
pain relief	il sollievo al dolore
vitamin supplements	i supplementi vitaminici
cure	la cura
homeopathic remedy	il rimedio omeopatico
exercise	l'esercizio
physiotherapy	la fisioterapia
rest	il riposo
sleep	il sonno
go to bed	va' / vada al letto
sleep	dormi / dorma
take more exercise	fa' / faccia del movimento
eat less	mangia / mangi di meno
avoid	evita / eviti

13.4 At the hospital

Core vocabulary

hospital	l'ospedale
department	il dipartimento / reparto
emergency	l'emergenza / urgenza
doctor	il medico
nurse	l'infermiera / l'infermiere
ward	la corsia / il reparto
bed	il letto
a health certificate	un certificato della salute
an examination	una visita
an x-ray	una radiografia
radiation	la radiazione
I have broken my leg / ankle / wrist ...	mi sono rotto la gamba / la caviglia / il polso
plaster	il gesso
crutches	le stampelle / grucce
walking stick	il bastone per camminare
wheel chair	la sedia a rotelle

anaesthetic	l'anestetico
surgery (medical procedure)	la chirurgia
surgery (place)	l'ambulatorio
operation	l'operazione / intervento chirurgico
operating theatre	la sala operatoria
family planning	la pianificazione familiare
contraception	la contraccezione
condom	il preservativo / profilattico
the coil	la spirale
the pill	la pillola
the morning after pill	la pillola del giorno dopo
vasectomy	la vasectomia

14

the world

14.1 Countries

Core vocabulary

the world	il mondo
the earth	la terra
the globe	il globo
the atlas	l'atlante
the continents	i continenti
Africa	l'Africa
America	l'America
North America	l'America del Nord
South America	l'America del Sud
Asia	l'Asia
Australia	l'Australia
Europe	l'Europa
the Arctic region	l'Artide
the Antarctica	l'Antartide
the Middle East	il Medio Oriente
the Far East	l'Estremo Oriente
the Pacific rim	la Costa del Pacifico
Indo-China	l'Indocina
India	l'India
China	la Cina
Japan	il Giappone
Indonesia	l'Indonesia
Australasia	Australia, Nuova Zelanda e Papua Nuova Guinea
New Zealand	la Nuova Zelanda
the Pacific Islands	le Isole del Pacifico

14.2 The countries of Europe

Core vocabulary

Europe	l'Europa
Scandinavia	la Scandinavia
Denmark	la Danimarca
Finland	la Finlandia
Norway	la Norvegia
Sweden	la Svezia
Iceland	l'Islanda
The Low Countries	i Paesi Bassi

Belgium	il Belgio
Holland	l'Olanda
Luxembourg	il Lussemburgo
the Iberian peninsula	la Penisola Iberica
Spain	la Spagna
Portugal	il Portogallo
the United Kingdom	il Regno Unito
England	l'Inghilterra
Scotland	la Scozia
Northern Ireland	l'Irlanda del Nord
Wales	il Galles
Greece	la Grecia
Turkey	la Turchia
Germany	la Germania
Poland	la Polonia
France	la Francia
Ireland	l'Irlanda
Austria	l'Austria
Italy	l'Italia
the Czech Republic	la Repubblica ceca
Hungary	l'Ungheria
Slovakia	la Slovacchia
Switzerland	la Svizzera
European Union	l'Unione Europea
European Parliament	il Parlamento Europeo
Common Market	il Mercato Comune
Member of the European Parliament	l'eurodeputato
common agricultural policy	la Politica Agricola Comune
Euro	l'euro
European institutions	le istituzioni europee
European bank	la Banca Europea

14.3 The high seas

the points of the compass *i punti cardinali*

north, north-east, north-west	nord, nord-est, nord-ovest
south, south-east, south-west	sud, sud-est, sud-ovest
east	est
west	ovest
the compass	la bussola

the oceans and the seas *gli oceani e i mari*

the Atlantic	l'Atlantico
the Indian	l'Oceano Indiano
the Pacific	il Pacifico
the Arctic	l'Artico
the Antartic	l'Antartico
the Mediterranean	il Mediterraneo
the North Sea	il mare del Nord
the Baltic	il (mar) Baltico
the Red Sea	il mar Rosso
the English Channel	il Canale della Manica
Ligurian Sea	il mar Ligure
Tyrrhenian Sea	il mar Tirreno
Adriatic Sea	il mar Adriatico
Ionian Sea	il mar Ionio
Bay of Naples / Salerno	il Golfo di Napoli / Salerno
Gulf of Genova / Taranto	il Golfo di Genova / Taranto
Straits of Messina	lo stretto di Messina
Sicily	la Sicilia
Sardinia	la Sardegna
Elba	l'isola d'Elba
navigation	la navigazione
longitude	la longitudine
latitude	la latitudine
equator	l'equatore
northern hemisphere	l'emisfero settentrionale
southern hemisphere	l'emisfero australe
tropics	i tropici
bay	la baia
island	l'isola
peninsula	la penisola
canal	il canale
Suez canal	il canale di Suez
Panama canal	il canale di Panama
straits	lo stretto
currents	le correnti
tides	le maree
ferry	il traghetto
liner	il transatlantico
cruise ship	la nave da crociera
tanker	la petroliera
container ship	la nave portacontainer

hazards	i pericoli
icebergs	gli iceberg
shipping	la navigazione
shipping forecast	il meteo per la navigazione marittima
storms	le tempeste / burrasche
gales	i venti forti / le burrasche
gale force (10)	il vento forza 10
rough seas	i mari molto mossi
calm seas	i mari calmi

Useful verbs

to board	salire a bordo (di)
to embark	imbarcarsi
to disembark	sbarcare

14.4 The weather forecast

Core vocabulary

rain	la pioggia
snow	la neve
wind	il vento
fog	la nebbia
sun	il sole
hail	la grandine
sleet	il nevischio
thunderstorm	il temporale
thunder	il tuono
lightening	il fulmine / lampo

What's the weather like? *Che tempo fa?*

It is … raining	piove / sta piovendo
snowing	nevica / sta nevicando
cloudy	è nuvoloso
overcast	è coperto
rainy	è piovoso
wet / damp / humid	è umido
sunny	c'è il sole
windy	c'è vento
mild	non fa freddo
a dry day	è un giorno senza pioggia

It is warm, hot	fa caldo, molto caldo
cold	fa freddo
good weather	fa bel tempo
bad weather	fa brutto tempo
yesterday	ieri
today	oggi
tomorrow	domani
over the next few days	nel corso dei prossimi giorni
the weather is getting worse	il tempo sta peggiorando
improving	migliorando

You can expect *Si può prevedere*

light / strong winds	venti leggeri / forti
rain / snow	pioggia / neve
clouds	nuvole
gusts of wind	raffiche di vento
gales	venti forti / bufere
storms	tempeste / burrasche
heavy showers	rovesci / acquazzoni
floods	inondazioni
sunny intervals	intervalli di sole
bright periods	intervalli sereni
prolonged spells of rain	periodi prolungati di pioggia
morning mist	nebbiolina mattuttina
fog patches	banchi di nebbia
frost	gelo / brina
dangerous driving conditions	condizioni delle strade pericolose per la guida
risk of flooding	rischio di inondazioni

the temperature *la temperatura*

degrees	gradi
Celsius/Centigrade	Celsius / centigrado
fahrenheit	Fahrenheit
the temperature is rising / falling	la temperatura sale / si abbassa
maximum	massimo
minimum	minimo

Radio weather forecast

Le previsioni meteorologiche per domani: nella parte nord della regione cielo molto nuvoloso e pioggia intermittente, venti molto deboli. Il cielo sarà sereno o poco nuvoloso sulla parte meridionale, ma farà più freddo, con venti inizialmente deboli da nordest, ma di pomeriggio venti più forti, mari da poco mosso a mosso, temperature minime 5, massime 15. Dopo domani arriveranno dei temporali e venti molto forti, forza 5 a 6.

Newspaper weather forecast

venerdì 21 marzo
Nord: parzialmente nuvoloso al mattino per nubi alte e stratiformi; banchi di nebbia al mattino sulla pianura; aumento della nuvolosità durante la giornata sull'estremo settore occidentale, con possibilità di locali piogge in serata. Centro: sereno o poco nuvoloso. Locali banchi di nebbia al primo mattino nelle vallate. Sud: poco nuvoloso con locali annuvolamenti più estesi nel corso della giornata sulle zone a ridosso dei rilievi. Temperature: senza variazioni di rilievo. Venti: deboli nord-orientali con locali rinforzi sulle zone adriatiche. Mari: poco mossi; localmente mosso l'Adriatico e lo Ionio.

15

government and society

15.1 Politics and government

Core vocabulary

government	il governo
democracy	la democrazia
rule of law	il principio di legalità
dictatorship	la dittatura
monarchy	la monarchia
UK's Parliamentary Monarchy	la monarchia parlamentare del Regno Unito
Italy's Republican Democracy	la democrazia repubblicana d'Italia

A brief overview of Italy's current political situation
Una visione d'insieme della situazione politica d'Italia

Italy's democratic state is a fairly typical republic, in that there are two parliamentary bodies – the House of Deputies and the Senate, both consisting of elected members; unusually, perhaps, Italy has both a President and a Prime Minister. An experienced politician can be elected to the role of president, but then rarely becomes involved directly in politics, having more of a figurehead role as Head of State. The Prime Minister, on the other hand, is the head of the government.

Italy has several main political parties, whose complex relationships have formed the many and usually short-lived governments of the last 60 years.

Democrazia Cristiana, which has most often formed the government, stands for conservative Christian values, a strong state, security and European commitment;

Partito Comunista Italiano, once the largest communist party in Europe and very influential, is now in decline.

Partito Socialista Italiano is a traditional Socialist party, standing for social justice and equality, but never ranking higher than third place.

Lega Nord was formed in 1989 to foster the interests of the prosperous north over the poorer south, and seeking independence from the rest of Italy.

In 2003, the Italian Royal Family, expelled from Italy when the Republic was formed in 1946 after World War II, was at long last allowed to visit Italy.

the Head of State	il Capo dello Stato
the President	il Presidente
the Prime Minister	il Primo Ministro
the King	il Re
the Queen	la Regina
the Royal Family	la Famiglia Reale
the Prince	il Principe
the Princess	la Principessa
to appoint one's government	nominare il governo
cabinet	il Consiglio dei Ministri
to appoint one's cabinet	nominare il Consiglio dei Ministri
the Minister of the Interior	il Ministro degli Interni
the Defence Minister	il Ministro della Difesa
the Chancellor of the Exchequer	il Ministro del Tesoro
the Justice Minister	il Ministro della Giustizia
parliament	il parlamento
chamber	la camera
Lower House (Italian Parliament)	la Camera dei Deputati
Upper House (Italian Parliament)	il Senato
member of lower house	il deputato
member of the higher chamber	il senatore
ministry	il ministero
Foreign Office	il Ministero degli Esteri
Home Office	il Ministero degli Interni
Ministry of Education	il Ministero della Pubblica Istruzione
Ministry of Defence	il Ministero della Difesa
the City council	il consiglio municipale
town hall	il municipio
town / city councillor	il consigliere municipale
mayor	il sindaco
constituency (area)	il collegio elettorale
election	le elezioni
the vote	il voto / la votazione
to speak	parlare
to make a speech	fare un discorso
to canvass	fare propaganda elettorale
to debate	dibattere / discutere

| to vote | votare |
| to pay taxes | pagare imposte / tasse |

the armed forces *le Forze Armate*

army	l'Esercito
soldier / tank / to march	il soldato / un carro armato / marciare
navy	la Marina (Militare)
sailor / warship / to sail	il marinaio / la nave da guerra / navigare
airforce	l'Aviazione Militare
airman / pilot / jet fighter / to fly	l'aviatore / il pilota / il caccia a reazione / volare
police force	la polizia
policeman / police car / to arrest	il poliziotto / la macchina della polizia / arrestare
war against terrorism	la guerra contro il terrorismo
war against organized crime	la guerra contro la criminalità organizzata
terrorist attack	l'attacco terrorista
suicide bomber	il terrorista suicida
sea to air missile	il missile mare-aria
to defend	difendere
to fight	combattere
to guard	fare la guardia a
to protect	proteggere
to spy	spiare

15.2 Local government and services

Core vocabulary

police	la polizia
emergency services	i servizi di pronto intervento
ambulance	l'ambulanza
fire brigade	il Corpo dei Vigili del Fuoco
telephone	il telefono
electricity	l'elettricità
gas	il gas
water	l'acqua
mayor	il sindaco
town hall	il municipio
local council	il consiglio comunale

roads	le strade
transport	i trasporti
tourist office	l'ufficio turistico
council offices	gli uffici municipali
telephone	il telefono
taxes	le imposte
council tax	l'imposta comunale
bureaucracy	la burocrazia
the small print	la parte scritta in piccolo
red tape	le lungaggini burocratiche
civil servant	il funzionario
paperwork	l'amministrazione
a pass	il lasciapassare
a permit	un permesso
a certificate of residence	un permesso di soggiorno
a receipt	una ricevuta
a driving licence	una patente di guida
insurance	l'assicurazione
medical insurance	l'assicurazione medica
medical check	la visita medica
solicitor / lawyer	l'avvocato / il notaio
criminal offence	il reato
court	il tribunale / la corte
sentence	la sentenza / condanna
fine	la multa
imprisonment	la reclusione

Useful phrases

I don't understand	Non capisco
I didn't know	Non lo sapevo
I have already supplied you with this document	Le ho già fornito questo documento
I need help ….	Ho bisogno di aiuto
Is there anyone who can help me?	C'è qualcuno che mi possa aiutare?
When are the offices open?	A che ora aprono gli uffici?
Where do I need to go to get …?	Dove devo andare per avere …?
What do I need?	Di che cosa ho bisogno?
Where can I get it?	Dove posso trovarlo/la?
a (rubber) stamp	il timbro
It has/hasn't been stamped	Non è stato timbrato

15.3 Money

currency	la moneta / valuta
dollars	i dollari
sterling	la sterlina
euros	gli euro
bank	la banca
bank account	il conto in banca
current account	il conto corrente
deposit	il deposito
saving account	il libretto di risparmio
account number	il numero del conto
bank sort code	il numero di agenzia bancaria
cash	contanti
a cheque	un assegno
cheque book	il libretto degli assegni
credit card	la carta di credito
cheque card	la carta assegni
signature	la firma
number / code	il numero / codice
loan	il prestito
overdraft	lo scoperto di conto
bank transfer	il trasferimento bancario / bonifico
in credit	coperto
in the red	scoperto / in rosso
bankruptcy	la bancarotta
mortgage	il mutuo ipotecario
household insurance	l'assicurazione sulla casa
to apply	presentare domanda
to be accepted	essere accettato
to be refused	essere rifiutato
stocks and shares	i valori di borsa
stock market	la borsa
prices	i prezzi
dividend	il dividendo
profits	i profitti
loss	la perdita
inflation	l'inflazione
to win	vincere
to lose	perdere
to make a gain	guadagnare

to make a loss	subire una perdita
to buy / sell shares	comprare / vendere azioni
to save	risparmiare
accounts	i conti
accountant	il ragioniere / commercialista
annual accounts	i conti annuali
income tax	l'imposta sul reddito

15.4 National holidays

national holidays	le feste nazionali
bank holidays	i giorni di feste civili
annual paid holidays	le ferie
local holidays	le feste locali
Christmas Eve	la Vigilia di Natale
Christmas Day	Natale
New Year's Eve	la Vigilia di Capodanno
New Year	il Capodanno
the Epiphany (6 January)	La Befana
Carnival	Carnevale
Shrove Tuesday	Martedì grasso
Ash Wednesday	Mercoledì delle Ceneri
Easter Week / Holy Week	(la) Settimana Santa
Good Friday	Venerdì Santo
Easter Sunday	Pasqua
Easter Monday	Pasquetta
Liberation Day (25 April)	La Liberazione
National Holiday (August 15)	Ferragosto
Halloween	la vigilia di Ognissanti
All Saints' Day	Ognissanti
feast of the Virgin Mary (8 December)	L'Immacolata
patron saint's day	la festa del santo patrono
village fete	la festa del paese
circus	il circo
concert	il concerto
band	la banda
gig	la serata musicale
festival of (music)	il festival (di musica)
competition	la gara
championship	il campionato
match	la partita

wine festival	la sagra del vino / della vendemmia
regional costume	il costume regionale
procession	la processione

15.5 Environmental issues

Core vocabulary

the environment	l'ambiente
environmentalist	l'ambientalista
environmental issues	le questioni ambientali
ecology	l'ecologia
ecosystem	l'ecosistema
erosion	l'erosione

foodstuffs *i generi alimentari*

GM (genetically modified)	geneticamente modificato
organic	organico
artificial fertilizer	il fertilizzante artificiale
nitrates	i nitrati
pesticides	il pesticida
poison	il veleno
weedkiller	l'erbicida

pollution *l'inquinamento*

environmental pollution	l'inquinamento ambientale
acid rain	la pioggia acida
air pollution	l'inquinamento atmosferico
car exhaust	i gas di scappamento delle macchine
detergent	il detergente / detersivo
biodegradable detergent	il detergente biodegradabile
global warming	il riscaldamento dell'atmosfera terrestre
greenhouse gas	l'effetto serra
nuclear testing	gli esperimenti nucleari
ozone layer	la fascia dell'ozono
radiation	la radiazione
radioactive waste	le scorie radioattive
water pollution	l'inquinamento dell'acqua

energy *l'energia*

power	l'elettricità / la corrente
nuclear power	l'energia nucleare
hydroelectric power	l'energia idroelettrica
solar power	l'energia solare
wind power	l'energia eolica
power station	la centrale elettrica

recycling *il riciclaggio*

glass	il vetro
cans	le scatole
paper	la carta
plastic	la plastica
compost	il concime

resources *le risorse*

sustainable resources	le risorse che possono essere mantenute
renewable	rinnovabile
Greenpeace	Greenpeace
the protection	la protezione
of the environment	dell'ambiente
of animals	degli animali
of plants	delle piante
to protect	proteggere
to conserve	conservare
to destroy	distruggere
to dispose of	disfarsi di
to throw away	buttare via / gettare
national park	il parco nazionale
region of special scientific interest	la regione di interesse scientifico speciale
protected / conservation area	la zona protetta
listed building	l'edificio protetto
ancient monument	il monumento storico
archeological site	i scavi archeologichi

15.6 Religion

Core vocabulary

| religion | la religione |
| beliefs | le credenze |

faith	la fede
Buddhism	il buddismo
Christianity	il cristianesimo
Hinduism	l'induismo
Islam	l'Islam

God	Dio
Buddha	Budda
Christ	Cristo
Mohammed	Maometto
the prophet	il profeta

I am a / an ...	sono ...
agnostic	agnostico
atheist	ateo
buddhist	buddista
catholic	cattolico
Christian	cristiano
Hindu	indù
Jew	ebreo
Moslem	musulmano
Quaker	quacchero
Jehovah's witness	Testimone di Geova

cathedral	il duomo / la cattedrale
chapel	la cappella
church	la chiesa
mosque	la moschea
temple	il tempio

religious leader	il capo religioso
bishop	il vescovo
imam	l'imam
monk	il frate / monaco
nun	la suora / monaca
priest	il prete / sacerdote
rabbi	il rabbino

prayer	la preghiera
hymn	l'inno
religious service	la funzione religiosa
mass	la messa
baptism, christening	il battesimo
(first) communion	la (prima) comunione
wedding	le nozze / il matrimonio
funeral	il funerale

Useful verbs

to *attend* church	andare in chiesa
to *believe*	credere
to *pray*	pregare
to *preach*	predicare
to *kneel*	inginocchiarsi
to *sing*	cantare / salmodiare
to *chant*	cantare
to *worship*	adorare

15.7 Social issues

Core vocabulary

the *community*	la comunità
charity / *charitable work*	le opere di carità
charity / *charitable organization*	l'organizzazione filantropica
social *services*	i servizi sociali
social *work*	l'assistenza sociale
the *quality of life*	la qualità della vita
fundamental *problems*	problemi fondamentali
financial *problems*	problemi finanziari
poverty	povertà / miseria
debt	debiti
psychological *problems*	i problemi psicologici
depression	la depressione
emotional *deprivation*	le carenze affettive
insecurity	l'insicurezza
loneliness	la solitudine
mental *health*	la salute mentale
neglect	la trascuratezza
racial *tension*	la tensione razziale
stress	lo stress / la tensione nervosa
unemployment	la disoccupazione
environmental *problems*	i problemi ambientali
bad *housing*	l'alloggio di bassa qualità
family *problems*	i problemi familiari
inner *city*	zona urbana in degrado
lack of *food* / clean water / sewage	la mancanza di cibo / acqua potabile / depurazione dei liquami

16

the media

16.1 The press

Core vocabulary

the press	la stampa
newspaper	il giornale
magazine, review	la rivista
comic	il giornalino a fumetti
daily	quotidiano
weekly	settimanale
monthly	mensile
bi-monthly	bimestrale
quarterly	trimestrale
yearly	annuale
publisher	la casa editrice
editor	il redattore
journalist	il giornalista
journalism	il giornalismo
reporter (press)	il reporter / cronista
reporter (TV, radio)	il telecronista
correspondent	il corrispondente
special correspondent	il corrispondente speciale
war correspondent	il corrispondente di guerra
critic	il critico
press agency*	l'agenzia stampa
Reuters	Reuters

*ANSA is a well-known Italian press agency.

front page	la prima pagina
back page	l'ultima pagina
headline	il titolo
column	la colonna
article	l'articolo
brief report	il reportage breve
advertisement	la pubblicità
TV advertisement	lo spot
notices	gli annunci
obituaries	i necrologi
small ads	gli annunci economici

news items *le notizie*

natural disaster	il disastro naturale
flood	l'inondazione
earthquake	il terremoto

201

the media

16

eruption of a volcano	l'eruzione di un vulcano
storm	la tempesta
hurricane	l'uragano
tornado	il tornado
torrential rain	la pioggia torrenziale
road accidents	gli incidenti stradali
car crash	l'incidente d'auto
collision	la collisione / lo scontro
plane crash	incidente aereo
a plane crashed over the Atlantic	un aereo è precipitato sopra l'Atlantico
boat involved in collision	nave coinvolta in una collisione
terrorist attack	l'attacco terrorista
demonstration	la manifestazione
strike	lo sciopero
a call to go on strike	la proclamazione di sciopero
fire	l'incendio
a fire started on the fourth level at 3 pm	un incendio è scoppiato al quarto piano alle ore 15

i

- Italian newspaper reports of incidents and accidents often use unexpected tenses; the present tense gives vividness to narration of incidents, and the imperfect is sometimes used with similar effect.

- The distinction in the British press between the tabloid press and the broad-sheet newspapers does not exist in Italy, where most papers are of the same size – smaller than a broad-sheet, but a bit larger than a tabloid paper. Of course, there are various sizes, but no division of style and tone as in the UK press.

- Newspapers in Italy tend to be focused on news rather than on gossip about stars and so on, which is left to magazines like *Oggi*, *Grazie*, *Ecco!* etc. As a rule, even regional papers contain lots of national and international news, as well as local news and information; as a result, many Italian people buy local rather than national papers.

16.2 Books

Core vocabulary

title	il titolo
author	l'autore / l'autrice

writer	lo scrittore / la scrittrice
illustrator	l'illustratore
cartoonist	il cartonista (di cartoni animati)
paperback	il tascabile / paperback
biography	la biografia
autobiography	l'autobiografia
novel	il romanzo
short story	il racconto / la novella
dictionary	il dizionario / vocabolario
encyclopaedia	l'enciclopedia
atlas	l'atlante
guide book	la guida turistica
(road) map book	l'atlante stradale
fiction	la narrativa
non-fiction	tutta la prosa che non è narrativa

the text *il testo*

to write	scrivere
to edit	curare / editare
to print	stampare
to publish	pubblicare
to sign	firmare
punctuation	la punteggiatura
paragraph	il paragrafo
sentence	la frase
line	la linea
capital / upper case letter	la maiuscola
lower case letter	la minuscola
full stop	il punto
comma	la virgola
semi-colon	il punto e virgola
colon	i due punti
exclamation mark	il punto esclamativo
question mark	il punto interrogativo
hyphen	il trattino
dash	la lineetta
dot-dot-dot	i puntini di sospensione

literary genres *i generi letterari*

novels	i romanzi
mystery novels	i romanzi del mistero
detective novels	i romanzi polizieschi / gialli
short stories	le novelle / i racconti
foreign literature	la letteratura straniera

literary review	la critica / recensione letteraria
poetry	la poesia
epic (poetry)	il poema epico
epic (film)	l'epopea
essays	i saggi*

i *This Italian word for a literary essay cannot be used in the school/student sense, when 'tema' or 'composizione' is used instead.

Useful phrases

What sort of books do you like to read?	Che genere di libro ti piace leggere?
Who is your favourite author?	Chi è il tuo autore preferito?
I like reading books about ...	Mi piace leggere dei libri su ...
I like reading books where ...	Mi piace leggere dei libri in cui ...
I like reading books that ...	Mi piace leggere dei libri che ...

16.3 Cinema and television

the cinema *il cinema*

auditorium	l'auditorio / la sala
(big) screen	lo schermo (grande)
seat	il posto
foyer	il ridotto / foyer
ticket	il biglietto
booking office	la biglietteria

types of films *generi di film*

thriller	il thriller
love story / romance	il film d'amore
historical film	il film di storia
science fiction	il film di fantascienza
horror film	il film dell'orrore
war film	il film di guerra
comedy	la commedia
detective	il film poliziesco
drama	il film drammatico
adverts	la pubblicità

the cast and the crew *il cast e la troupe*

| a film star | un divo del cinema |

an actor / actress	un attore / un'attrice
a leading role	un ruolo di primo piano
a supporting role	un ruolo non di protagonista
a singer	un/una cantante
a dancer	un ballerino / una ballerina
director	il regista
producer	il produttore / la produttrice
cameraman	il cameraman
sound recordist	il tecnico del suono

television *la televisione*

television set	il televisore
small screen	lo schermo piccolo
cable	televisione via cavo
satellite	televisione via satellite
dish	l'antenna parabolica
video recorder	il videoregistratore
dvd recorder	il lettore-registratore DVD
video rental / shop	la videoteca
the video	il video
the DVD	il DVD
the film is dubbed / subtitled	questo film è doppiato / hai sottotitoli
remote control	il telecomando
channel	il canale

the programmes *i programmi*

credits (opening / closing)	i titoli di testa /coda
commercials (adverts)	gli spot
cartoons	i cartoni animati
children's programmes	i programmi per bambini
chat show	il talk show
documentary	il documentario
feature film	il lungometraggio
game show	il gioco a premi
quiz programme	il programma di quiz
news programme	il programma di notizie
opinion programme	un dibattito televisivo
soap	la telenovela / soap opera
weather forecast	le previsioni del tempo / il meteo

the people *le persone*

news reporter	il reporter
news reader	l'annunciatore / l'annunciatrice

presenter	il presentatore / la presentatrice
interviewer	l'intervistatore / l'intervistatrice
commentator	il radiocronista / telecronista
disc jockey	il DJ / disc jockey
game show host	il presentatore di un gioco a premi
the viewer	il telespettatore / la telespettatrice

radio *la radio*

station	la stazione
programme	il programma
frequency	la frequenza
on FM	FM / a modulazione di frequenza
on LW	in onde lunghe
on MW	in onde medie

Useful verbs

to *change channels*	cambiare di canale
to *turn on / off the telly*	accendere / spegnere la tivù
to *turn the sound up*	alzare il volume
to *turn the sound down*	abbassare il volume
to *broadcast*	trasmettere
to *record*	registrare

Useful phrases

What is your favourite programme?	Qual è il tuo programma preferito?
Do you like documentaries?	Ti piacciono i documentari?
Who is your favourite presenter?	Chi è il tuo presentatore preferito?
He/she is partial / impartial	(Lei/lui) è parziale / imparziale

taking it further

Books

For an introduction to Italian history, geography, language and culture, and modern-day society, try:

Teach Yourself Italian Language, Life & Culture, Derek Aust with Mike Zollo (Hodder and Stoughton, 2003).
Modern Italy 1871–1995, Martin Clark (Longman, 1996).

For those wanting more in-depth knowledge of the language:

The Italian Language Today, Anna and Giulio Lepschy (Routledge, 1988).
A Linguistic History of Italian, Martin Maiden (Longman, 1995).

Watching and listening

Satellite television is a good investment – in the UK, many Italian television stations are available on Eutelsat FII / Hotbird. In some areas, Italian channels are available on Cable TV.

Radio reception on a normal set is variable, though in some areas Italian stations can be received clearly, depending on atmospheric conditions. Many good Italian radio stations are available on Satellite TV. For Italian music, try **Radio Italia S** *(solo musica italiana)* on the Hotbird satellite, which only broadcasts Italian music.

If you can access Italian television or radio, listen to a variety of different types of material or programmes. Try watching or listening to the news having already seen or heard it in the

English-speaking media, as many international news items will be shown on both. This will help your understanding and give you confidence.

If you are interested in opera or popular music, choose recordings with clear lyrics; in the case of opera, the names of Luciano Pavarotti and Andrea Bocelli are well known. Italian popular music features many *cantautori* – singer-song-writers – and their ballad-style songs can offer good listening practice. CDs are easily available in Italy, but a specialist music shop may also be able to help. Try some of the following: **Luigi Tenco, Gino Paoli, Fabrizio de André, Lucio Battisti, Lucio Dalla, Paolo Conte.** If you prefer more of a 'rock' style, try **Luciano Ligabue, Litfiba** and **Edoardo Bennato.** Finally, the internationally known **Zucchero (Sugar) Fornaciari** has many slowish ballads in his repertoire in which the diction is clear enough to make for pleasurable and instructive listening.

Many Italian films are available on video and DVD, most with English sub-titles if you really need them!

Places to go

Look out for performances of Italian culture in local venues, for example, opera, films, art exhibitions, etc. Also watch out for Italian (speaking) films at local film clubs and on television.

Italian paintings are sometimes displayed in galleries outside Italy, including the USA and UK. Often, there are special seasons, when Italian works of art are brought for short-term exhibitions.

Reading

Obviously, this will depend on whether or not you can read Italian well enough to keep your interest going! Try short, simple items in the press, such as advertisements, small ads and short articles on well-known subjects. Another very useful source of reading material is the Internet, where there is plenty of visual material to support your understanding. Try tourist and hotel websites, or go to one which deals with your hobby or your work specialization: you will already know a lot about the topic, so even understanding new words will be easier as you are familiar with the context.

If you wish to read literature in Italian, the best approach is to go for a 'school text' if one is available, that is one which has been set for Italian literature examinations: such editions have a useful introduction, explanatory notes and glossaries.

Websites

The web is very popular in Italy and is very widely used, so there is plenty of good material available in Italian – all good practice. Choose your subject and do the necessary search, but be prepared to be bombarded with Italian. There are Italian websites available related to many of the subjects covered in this book. You can either and do a search using your favourite English-language search engine, preferably one with Italian links, or if you can cope with the language enough to use an Italian search engine, go direct to one of those listed below.

Be warned: websites come and go, and their addresses often change. These were all fine at the time of going to press!

Search engines

http://www.virgilio.it
http://arianna.libero.it/

Using an Italian search engine may speed up your search for a specific Italian site.

Tourism, culture and current affairs

http://www.italyguide.com
http://www.lonelyplanet.com/destinations/europe/italy/
http://www.initaly.com
http://www.italcultur.org.uk

The press

Corriere della Sera   http://corriere.virgilio.it
Il Mattino   http://www.ilmattino.it

Language learning on the web

For basic language practice, go to:

http://www.languagesonline.org.uk
http://www.bbc.co.uk/education/languages
http://polyglot.lss.wisc.edu/lss/lang/teach.html

Italian Embassies

The Italian Embassies in London and Washington provide many services online and links to other useful Internet sites:

http://www.embitaly.org.uk
http://www.italyemb.org

teach yourself

italian
lydia vellaccio & maurice elston

- Do you want to cover the basics then progress fast?
- Have you got rusty Italian which needs brushing up?
- Do you want to reach a high standard?

Italian starts with the basics but moves at a lively pace to give you a good level of understanding, speaking and writing. You will have lots of opportunity to practise the kind of language you will need to be able to communicate with confidence and understand the culture of speakers of Italian.

teach
yourself

italian grammar
anna proudfoot

- Are you looking for an accessible guide to Italian grammar?
- Do you want a book you can use either as a reference or as a course?
- Would you like exercises to reinforce your learning?

Italian Grammar explains the most important structures in a clear and jargon-free way, with plenty of examples to show how they work in context. Use the book as a comprehensive reference to dip in and out of or work through it to build your knowledge.

teach
yourself

italian verbs
maria bonacina

- Do you want a handy reference to check verb forms?
- Are you finding tenses difficult?
- Do you want to see verbs used in a variety of contexts?

Italian Verbs is a quick and easy way to check the form and
meaning of over 3500 verbs. The clear layout makes the book
very easy to navigate and the examples make the uses clear at
the same time as building your vocabulary.

teach yourself

world cultures: italy
derek aust with mike zollo

- Are you interested in the story of Italy and the Italians?
- Do you want to understand how the country works today?
- Are you planning a visit to Italy or learning Italian?

World Cultures: Italy will give you a basic overview of Italy – the country, its language, its people and its culture – and will enrich any visit or course of study. Vocabulary lists and 'Taking it Further' sections at the end of every chapter will equip you to talk and write confidently about all aspects of Italian life.

teach yourself®

the A-Z of teach yourself language titles

Afrikaans
Arabic
Arabic Script, Beginner's
Bengali
Brazilian Portuguese
Bulgarian
Cantonese
Catalan
Chinese
Chinese, Beginner's
Chinese Language, Life & Culture
Chinese Script, Beginner's
Croatian
Czech
Danish
Dutch
Dutch, Beginner's
Dutch Dictionary
Dutch Grammar
English, American (EFL)
English as a Foreign Language
English, Correct
English Grammar
English Grammar (EFL)
English, Instant, for French Speakers
English, Instant, for German Speakers
English, Instant, for Italian Speakers
English, Instant, for Spanish Speakers
English for International Business
English Language, Life & Culture
English Verbs
English Vocabulary
Finnish
French
French, Beginner's
French Grammar
French Grammar, Quick Fix
French, Instant
French, Improve your
French Language, Life & Culture
French Starter Kit
French Verbs

French Vocabulary
Gaelic
Gaelic Dictionary
German
German, Beginner's
German Grammar
German Grammar, Quick Fix
German, Instant
German, Improve your
German Language, Life & Culture
German Verbs
German Vocabulary
Greek
Greek, Ancient
Greek, Beginner's
Greek, Instant
Greek, New Testament
Greek Script, Beginner's
Gulf Arabic
Hebrew, Biblical
Hindi
Hindi, Beginner's
Hindi Script, Beginner's
Hungarian
Icelandic
Indonesian
Irish
Italian
Italian, Beginner's
Italian Grammar
Italian Grammar, Quick Fix
Italian, Instant
Italian, Improve your
Italian Language, Life & Culture
Italian Verbs
Italian Vocabulary
Japanese
Japanese, Beginner's
Japanese, Instant
Japanese Language, Life & Culture
Japanese Script, Beginner's
Korean

Latin
Latin American Spanish
Latin, Beginner's
Latin Dictionary
Latin Grammar
Nepali
Norwegian
Panjabi
Persian, Modern
Polish
Portuguese
Portuguese, Beginner's
Portuguese Grammar
Portuguese, Instant
Portuguese Language, Life & Culture
Romanian
Russian
Russian, Beginner's
Russian Grammar
Russian, Instant
Russian Language, Life & Culture
Russian Script, Beginner's
Sanskrit
Serbian
Spanish
Spanish, Beginner's
Spanish Grammar
Spanish Grammar, Quick Fix
Spanish, Instant
Spanish, Improve your
Spanish Language, Life & Culture
Spanish Starter Kit
Spanish Verbs
Spanish Vocabulary
Swahili
Swahili Dictionary
Swedish
Tagalog
Teaching English as a Foreign Language
Teaching English One to One
Thai
Turkish
Turkish, Beginner's
Ukrainian
Urdu
Urdu Script, Beginner's
Vietnamese
Welsh
Welsh Dictionary
Welsh Language, Life & Culture
Xhosa
Zulu

available from bookshops and on-line retailers

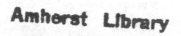